"I like the way Larry Winget practices tough love. He doesn't tell you what you want to hear so you'll feel warm and fuzzy; he tells you what you need to hear so you'll feel uncomfortable and improve your life. So do yourself a favor and read this book."

—Mark Sanborn, bestselling author of *The Fred Factor* and *You Don't Need a Title to Be a Leader*

"There's only one person in the world who could write this book. And lucky for you—he did. I dare you to read it. You may love it. You might hate it. But read it."

—Randy Gage, author of the *New York Times* bestseller *Risky Is the New Safe*

"Larry Winget is the perfect balance of you 'get over yourself' and 'take responsibility.' You don't have an ounce of breathing space to be less than, blame, or wait for success. This is why no one has the ability to get you fast results in your life or business like Larry. Few books can kick your butt so far so fast."

—Suzanne Evans, bestselling author of *The Way You Do Anything Is the Way You Do Everything*

"Winget emboldens readers to blaze a path through life with a strong sense of purpose, self-possession, and the ability to learn from criticism and failure."

—*Publishers Weekly*

"A fast read with powerful messages and easy concepts."   —Examiner.com

"Read [Winget's] gripping advice, and you won't roll over and play dead ever again."

—United Feature Syndicate

"Consider me a raving fan."

—RevivingWorkEthic.com

"An in-your-face, take-no-prisoners book for those who know they need a little bit of the plain truth . . . and especially for those who don't. It's a book that I needed to read . . . and I'll bet that you do, too."
—McKainViewpoint.com

"It has never been more important for you to stand up for yourself and your rights. In *Grow a Pair*, Larry explains practical strategies for protecting yourself, your family, and our country!"
—Grant Cardone, TV's Turnaround King

© PHYLLIS LANE

Larry Winget is the author of *New York Times* and *Wall Street Journal* bestsellers including *Your Kids Are Your Own Fault*, *The Idiot Factor*, *You're Broke Because You Want to Be*, *It's Called Work for a Reason*, and *Shut Up, Stop Whining, and Get a Life*. Known to his fans as the Pitbull of Personal Development®, he is one of the country's leading business speakers and a member of the International Speaker Hall of Fame. He has more than twenty years of experience speaking to nearly four hundred of the Fortune 500, sharing his insights and principles in the areas of success, leadership, customer service, sales, and personal finance. Larry coached families in financial crisis on A&E's reality series *Big Spender*, and he is a featured expert on many television shows including Fox News, CNBC, and others.

GROW A PAIR

How to Stop Being a Victim and Take Back Your Life, Your Business, and Your Sanity

LARRY WINGET

GOTHAM BOOKS

GOTHAM BOOKS
Published by the Penguin Group
Penguin Group (USA) LLC
375 Hudson Street
New York, New York 10014

USA | Canada | UK | Ireland | Australia
New Zealand | India | South Africa | China

penguin.com
A Penguin Random House Company

Previously published as a Gotham Books hardcover

First trade paperback printing, August 2014

3   5   7   9   10   8   6   4

Gotham Books and the skyscraper logo are trademarks of
Penguin Group (USA) LLC

Copyright © 2013 by Larry Winget

The Library of Congress has catalogued
the hardcover edition of this book as follows:

Winget, Larry.
Grow a pair: how to stop being a victim and take back your life, your business,
and your sanity / Larry Winget.
pages   cm
ISBN 978-1-592-40846-7 (HC)   978-1-592-40855-9 (Pbk)
1. Assertiveness (Psychology)   2. Self-actualization (Psychology)   I. Title.
BF575.A85W56 2013
158.2—dc23   2013016263

Printed in the United States of America
Set in Janson Text · Designed by Spring Hoteling

Art by Shane Closter

I dedicate this book to the men and women of the
United States military, and all those who serve us proudly
in our police and fire departments across our great country.

It is better to live one day as a tiger
than to live for a thousand years as a sheep.

—Tibetan Proverb

CONTENTS

PREFACE

Grow a pair. You've heard that phrase before and chances are you know exactly what it means. However, in case you live under a rock and the phrase and its meaning have somehow escaped you, here is the definition according to the *Urban Dictionary*: "Telling someone they don't have the balls to do something they know they should be doing." And the *Urban Dictionary*'s thesaurus gives us these substitutions for "grow a pair": to man up, cowboy up, quit being a pussy, and get the sand out of your vajayjay.

A pair obviously means balls. But don't be sophomoric and turn this into some grade school sexual thing. I'm not talking about testicles or physical balls; I'm talking about mental balls. And by the way, if you guys think you are the only ones with balls, you are wrong. Growing a pair has nothing to do with masculine versus feminine. I can show you lots of men who have balls, yet have no *balls*. I can also show you lots of women who have a bigger pair than most men can ever hope to have. So here, in the first few hundred

words of this little book, get past the physical and the
sexual and get your giggles out of the way, and then
let's talk about what growing a pair really means.

I have written five bestsellers, so you would think I
would have pretty much covered this problem by now
in my other books, wouldn't you? You would think that
a book entitled *Shut Up, Stop Whining, and Get a Life*
would have covered this. Or maybe *People Are Idiots and
I Can Prove It!* Wouldn't that one cover this topic?
Those books, along with my others—*It's Called Work
for a Reason!; You're Broke Because You Want to Be; No
Time for Tact;* and *Your Kids Are Your Own Fault*—are
tactical books. Great books, by the way, but they don't
deal with *this* issue. Those books each lay out a specific
problem, then provide the reader with simple, straight-
forward tactics that can be used to deal with and solve
the problem. This problem isn't that easy. This problem isn't as tactical. Yes, there are specific tactics you
can implement and take action on to grow a pair and
I'm going to give them to you in just a few pages. But
the tactics alone aren't enough to really grow a pair.
This problem is about creating an entirely new mind-
set. It's about a new way of thinking. It's about a new
way of living. In other words, growing a pair has nothing to do with what's between your legs and everything
to do with what's between your ears.

Growing a pair is a state of mind, an attitude, and
a way of thinking. It's about giving up being a victim
and taking control of your life at every level. It is the

willingness to do the right thing even when everyone else is doing the wrong thing. It has its roots in personal responsibility, accountability, confidence, and integrity. It's about establishing a standard by which you will live your life. It's about drawing lines in the sand. It's about knowing yourself, knowing your values, and becoming uncompromising in your willingness to do whatever it takes to stand up for them.

After reading that last paragraph, don't you agree that our society is in desperate need of developing that mind-set? Don't you believe that most folks are in need of a pair?

Those who stand for nothing fall for anything.

—Alexander Hamilton

THE PROBLEM

We have become a society of weenies. I hate admitting that, but since I am not a weenie, I will. For the most part, people are weak, sniveling, whining, backstabbing, gossiping, spineless weenies and let other people walk all over them.

People deliver bad service and we take it without ever saying anything about it. We allow friends to say hurtful things to us, without saying a word in our own defense. We let our government—people we elect and whose salaries we pay—take advantage of us, instead of fighting back by voting them out. We sit in theaters and let people text, take phone calls, and talk loudly to each other like they are sitting in their own living rooms, and most of us never bother to speak up and tell them to shut the hell up. We watch people throw their trash in the street or parking lot and never say a word to them.

Businesses now seem to be run by bad employees with poor work habits and lousy attitudes because their manager doesn't have the guts to discipline them or fire their lazy butts. And in many cases, HR departments won't let management do their job of actually managing their employees for fear of a lawsuit from some nitwit who might sue because their fragile feelings got hurt when they were told to get back to work. It's insane!

The popular network television show *What Would You Do?* puts people in the dilemma of "should I intervene?" when they see people being robbed, or property being vandalized, or other scandalous behavior. Sadly, most people don't speak up even when witnessing a crime because they just can't be bothered, don't want to make waves, or because they are afraid.

All of this has to stop. People need to speak up, step up, and behave boldly! We need to update and personalize the great line from Virgil's *Aeneid*, "Audentes fortuna juvat!"—"Fortune favors the bold!"

Standing up for yourself is no longer a part of what we teach people. Instead, we teach people to go along and get along. We encourage passiveness in our responses to bullies, to stupidity, and to corruption. We tolerate poor performance, bad service, inappropriate behavior, and other unacceptable practices. We have made being nice and being liked more important than being respected. Assertiveness is frowned upon. Having a strong opinion is no longer the way to go because you are considered an extremist; straddling the fence is much more popular.

Yet when any of this lousy behavior happens and

actually affects our lives, people whine that they are being taken advantage of. Of course they are! People are allowing this poor behavior. They are allowing themselves to be run over and can't seem to figure out how it is happening to them. You're standing in the middle of the road—move!

All of this must stop. We all need to grow a pair, act with assertiveness, speak up for ourselves, take a stand, and refuse to accept less than the best from others or from ourselves.

PICTURE THIS.

Imagine a society where people do the right thing every time. A world where every person is honest and has integrity and keeps their word. Where we show up on time. Where we respect others, their time, their property, their opinion. Picture a world where people are responsible and hold others accountable.

Imagine businesses where employees do their job because it is the right thing to do. Where we are more interested in doing a good job than seeing how much work we can get out of without being caught. Where we treat customers well and provide amazing service because we understand that the customer has the money that keeps us paid and our company in business. A world where employers treat their employees with dignity and respect and where employees are grateful for their jobs and are committed to excellence. Where both groups create a team committed to serving customers.

Imagine a government where politicians tell the truth and deliver on their promises. Where they run honest campaigns with no mudslinging. Where they refuse to compromise their beliefs or pander to special interest groups in order to get more funding for their campaigns and for votes. Where we once again look up to our elected officials as people we can believe in, who want to serve their constituents and not spend all of their time making decisions just so they can be re-elected.

Imagine a world where parents are less concerned with being their kid's friend, and more concerned with raising responsible, productive adults, which means stepping up to the plate and making the tough, unpopular parenting decisions. Where parents set good examples for their kids by spending their money on things that matter and teaching their kids about money. Where parents read, exercise, eat right, play with their kids, and openly communicate about relationships, sex, bullying, and the sensitive topics that in reality they too often avoid.

Is all of this too much to ask? Probably. Will all of it happen? Definitely not. But that doesn't mean we shouldn't try. That doesn't mean that we should become complacent and just maintain the status quo because creating this world takes too much effort.

How do we create a world like the one I just

described? We need every person to do his part. Remember: You can't change the world, but you can change *your* world. And if enough people commit to changing their world and teaching their kids what it takes to live this kind of life, then the world will be a different place.

This is a biggie (I like to give warnings if I have a biggie so you won't miss it!):

FIX YOURSELF FIRST!

That's right—work on you before you concern yourself with other folks. Remember that people change when they want to and not when you want them to, so instead of worrying yourself with fixing everyone else, focus on fixing yourself. When you think you've mastered a bit of this stuff, then move on to your kids and teach them. Then communicate with the people you come in contact with every day to educate them on your new view. Most importantly, live like you have a pair and set a good example so it will rub off on those around you!

CHECK YOURSELF
BEFORE YOU WRECK YOURSELF.

When everyone gets it but you, it's probably you, not it.

—Larry Winget

Let's face it: I have offended some of you already. Before we even get started, you're ticked off at me and the premise of the book. Maybe it's the crass title or the innuendo that's implied. Maybe it's the picture on the cover, or my shirt or my earrings.

Some of you are going to be offended by my choice of words as you read, saying that they are profane. Grow up. (Or perhaps just do what the book title says and grow a pair.)

And please don't bother giving me any of your "But Larry, you don't understand; I am the exception to what you just said." I am tired of people coming up with all of the exceptions to everything I write. *Of course* there are exceptions. Very few things come without an exception of some kind. It is impossible for me to write a blog, a Facebook post, a tweet, or a book that deals with every individual's personal issues. I can't write something that applies to 99 percent of the people while catering to you, the 1 percent. I don't care that you were a middle child born in North Dakota of parents named Lester and Josephine who made exactly $42,936 a year, and you had an older sister with red hair, a bucktoothed little brother with Tourette's syndrome, and a pet rabbit named Floppy, and because of all of that, you don't have any choice about your life and you can't be healthy or rich or successful. Yet that seems to be what some of you expect.

Besides, I have discovered that those who consider themselves to be the exception to the rule should re-read the rule.

Those who consider themselves to be the exception to the rule should re-read the rule.

And for those of you who just read everything I wrote here and are now saying "how dare you," I dare because I actually have a pair.

DO YOU HAVE A PAIR?

ANSWER THESE QUESTIONS:

- Do you allow people to take advantage of you?
- Do your kids talk back to you?
- Do you find yourself picking up the slack for lazy coworkers?
- Do you let people cut in front of you in line?
- Do you accept bad service without speaking up?
- Do you eat cold food in a restaurant rather than send it back?
- Do you allow people you are paying to be late for appointments?
- Do you let things slide even though it bothers you?
- Do you let your friends hurt your feelings, and never say a word about it?
- Do you often feel responsible for other people and their feelings?

- Do you find yourself unwilling to express yourself for fear of offending someone?
- Do you ever feel that people don't respect you?
- Do you find yourself compromising your opinions and beliefs in an effort to get along?
- Do you ever feel like you are being used?
- Do people talk down to you?
- Do people mistreat you emotionally, verbally, psychologically, or physically?

If you answered yes to any of these questions, chances are pretty good that you don't have a pair. If you read these questions and respond with anything even close to "yeah, Larry, but you don't understand!" and then offer up explanations about why you let people get by with this kind of stuff, then you don't have a pair. People who have a pair don't offer up excuses or explanations. They face the facts, take responsibility, and deal with the consequences. And they don't put up with any of this crap!

GIVE THIS LIST OF QUESTIONS A TRY:

- Do you stand up for yourself and your beliefs even in the face of conflict?
- Do you feel in control of your life?

- Do you feel a sense of purpose and determination when you wake up in the morning?
- Do you recognize your problems as problems but know that with some hard work and a little sweat you will get through them?
- When faced with overwhelming adversity, do you suck it up and go to work on it?
- Are you confident in your ability to deal with the challenges of life?
- When you make a mistake, do you take responsibility for your actions?
- Do you speak up when you see someone else being mistreated?
- When you get bad service, do you complain politely and make your grievances known?

If you answered yes to this set of questions, then congratulations—you have a pair.

WHERE DID EVERYONE'S PAIR GO?

People used to have a pair. I know that my generation (baby boomers) had a pair. At least they did when they were younger. It's the reason my generation was the most productive in recent history. And our parents' generation had a pair. They didn't take crap off of anyone. If you were rude or insulting, someone knocked you on your ass. If you talked back to your mama, you got it from her and then from your daddy too. If you got in trouble at school, your parents didn't sue the teacher or the school; they knew you were the problem and held you accountable. If you got bullied at school, your folks taught you how to stand up for yourself, and the teachers let you work it out between yourselves with little or no interference. If at work you lied or were late too many times, you got fired. If as a country you attacked us, we held you accountable and went to war and kicked your ass.

So what happened? Where did our collective pair go? I believe we got castrated by the new age, smiley face, psychobabble, positive thinking, hug it out, you're special, you-can-do-anything crowd that has become so popular.

The first I can remember of it all started back in the late sixties with Thomas Harris's book, *I'm OK—You're OK*. I find the truth to be closer to "I'm not that great, but you really suck!" Then the hippies took up the mantra with the *love* generation—and stupid sayings like "it's copacetic." The Jamaicans have their version: "No problem, man." Well, it's not copacetic and there *is* a problem. Beatniks and then hippies said, "Be cool." Big mistake. We went from "be responsible" to "be cool" and things fell apart.

Somewhere along the way with this line of

thinking we reached a place where we were supposed to just let people be idiots and not worry about it. We stopped holding people accountable for their mistakes to the point where we enabled them and bailed them out. We got soft. When faced with irresponsibility and stupidity, we told people to "let it slide." Well, we did let it slide and it slid straight into the toilet!

Add all of this irresponsibility together with some good old government money and you end up with the most entitled, pairless society in history. I doubt there is anyone at this point, regardless of your politics, who can make an intelligent argument against the fact that we have become the society with the biggest sense of entitlement in the history of our world. I have written much about the problems of entitlement in each of my bestselling books and have talked about it for years in blogs and social media and on various television shows. We are the entitlement generation. In fact, roughly 60 percent of all government spending is for a series of programs that are—by name— *entitlement programs*. This is not a partisan problem; both sides facilitated this issue. So don't go screaming about the Democrats or the Republicans. This is not the time to blame a political party, as this is not just a government issue. This is a people issue. People want to be taken care of and don't care who pays for it as long as it's not them!

People actually believe they are owed a living while doing nothing on their own to make sure they are employed or have any savings or that their bills are paid. That's why we have sixth generation welfare recipients. Folks believe they are owed retirement income, even though they spent every dime they had their entire working lives with little or no thought about what would happen when they were finally put out to pasture or if their company went out of business. People think they are owed unending unemployment benefits, when they did nothing to put away any money for a rainy day and make little effort to become reemployed. And the evidence shows that many didn't even do the work they were being paid for in the first place when they still had a job. Most of the Ninety-Nine Weekers (those folks who receive unemployment benefits for the maximum ninety-nine weeks) never even bother to look for a job until the last few weeks before their unemployment runs out.

Many believe they are owed healthcare benefits regardless of the fact that they destroyed their own health by smoking or overeating, usually both. Or they drink too much and have a car accident and then sue the bartender. Some folks wear the latest fashions, have big-screen televisions, drive a new car, and eat every meal at a restaurant and yet they have never bothered to save a dime. Then they blame others once they are broke and they want—no, *expect*—the rest of us to take care of them.

Bottom line: People believe they are entitled to compensation for consequences they brought on themselves due to their irresponsible lifestyle and stupid choices.

How did this happen? How did we reach this point? My parents' generation didn't think this way. Yet they raised the baby boomers who created this mess. And now the baby boomers have raised a generation with an even bigger sense of entitlement. And the next generation already looks like it's going to be even worse: Have you seen the Occupy movement?

I just finished reading the *New York Times* bestseller *World War Z* by Max Brooks. I ran across this great line: "You can blame the politicians, the businessmen, the generals, the 'machine,' but really, if you're looking to blame someone, blame me. I'm the American system, I'm the machine. That's the price of living in a democracy; we all gotta take the rap. . . . Nice to be able to say, 'Hey, don't look at me, it's not my fault.' Well, it is. It is my fault, and the fault of everyone of my generation."

Thank you, Max Brooks. I couldn't agree more. It's everyone's fault. I could sum up all that I teach, speak, and write about in one sentence: Life is your own damn fault.

But let's get back to that nagging question: What happened to the baby boomers to move them from being self-sufficient like their parents to becoming so self-indulgent? There are several answers to this problem but I would like to start with the self-help movement.

SHOULD WE BLAME THE SELF-HELP MOVEMENT?

Before the baby boomers, there wasn't a self-help movement; there was only the "help yourself" movement. The baby boomers created and went like lemmings into the sea of "positive thinking" rallies. We created bestsellers like Norman Vincent Peale's *You Can If You Think You Can* and *The Power of Positive Thinking*, and Napoleon Hill's *Think and Grow Rich*. And we took a pots-and-pans salesman named Zig Ziglar and turned him into the king of motivational speakers. Then we created an entire industry of motivational speakers like Tony Robbins, Jim Rohn, Earl Nightingale, and yes, even Larry Winget. Some added a religious element and put Jesus into the equation and we ended up with Robert Schuller and now Joel Osteen. Then we pushed the whole concept even further and ended up with books like *The Secret* and *The Law of Attraction* and folks started following abominations with messiah complexes like James Ray. You can say what you like about what I do for a living, but no one ever died as a result of attending a Larry Winget seminar. And I won't make you walk on fire or sit in a sweat lodge. I'll just ask you to look in an imaginary mirror and take responsibility for the life you have created. If that kills you, your reflection must be pretty bad!

So is the self-help industry a bad thing? And what

about Zig Ziglar and Norman Vincent Peale and Earl Nightingale and Tony Robbins and the thousands of other motivational speakers yelling positive platitudes from stages all over the world—are they bad? No. I like much of what the motivational guys do. Not all of it for sure, but much of it. So let's make it clear: I am *not* blaming the messenger. And I am not blaming the message. The message itself isn't bad at all, but we have bastardized the message and ended up producing the exact opposite result of the original intent. The original intent was to get people to realize that they had the power, all within themselves, to change their results. It was meant to give them the confidence to go out and work and use their talents to create success, happiness, and prosperity. It was a message meant to empower people to become all that they had the potential of becoming. That message of empowerment is important and necessary and powerful. Sadly, that message has been twisted and corrupted and in many cases, lost.

WE TURNED EMPOWERMENT INTO ENTITLEMENT.

Zig Ziglar said, "You can be whatever you want to be, do whatever you want to do, and have whatever you want to have as long as you believe in yourself." That statement was meant to empower people to have confidence in themselves and to believe in their abilities to work and achieve their goals and aspirations. And we messed it up. It might have been our laziness that messed it up, or our ever-declining work ethic, or our sliding scale of morality, or the gray area of integrity that runs rampant among workers, corporations, Wall Street, and government. Add to that our greed and unhealthy desire for more and *more* and *MORE*. Maybe it's our demand for more sensationalism via our insatiable need to be entertained. Or maybe it's our fascination with the shallow, inane, and ridiculous. But whatever happened, it corrupted the entire self-help movement. Somehow the self-help movement shifted from *self*, which was the original message, to *help*.

What's the solution? Stop thinking about *help* and turn back to your *self*. Stop blaming others. Stop looking to others to save you. Don't be a follower of the ideas of any individual, group, party, church, or other movement. Instead, you should read, study, think, and *work*. Rely on your brain and your brawn to create the life you want. In other words: *Grow a pair!*

WE GAVE IN TO POLITICAL CORRECTNESS.

While there is a lot of blame to spread around when it comes to our lack of having a pair, one of the most castrating effects on our society is political correctness.

Let me give you some examples of how ridiculous political correctness has become. And remember, we allowed this to happen.

There was a recent ruling in New York City public schools that tests given to students could not contain these words: birthday, Halloween, poverty, politics, aliens, computer, dancing, any reference to homes with swimming pools, and any reference to disease.

In 2007, hired Santa Clauses in Sydney, Australia, were forced to revolt for the right to say "ho, ho, ho," which is the traditional laugh of Santa Claus. They were told that "ho, ho, ho" could frighten children and could be considered derogatory to women. After all, we all know that ho is a "ho," right? Instead, they were instructed to say "ha, ha, ha."

And look at what has happened to our language:

A "criminal" is now "behaviorally challenged."

It is being suggested that we never call a person a "failure" but instead refer to that state as "deferred success."

We even have a twenty-four-term congressman who says that people who are living in the United States illegally aren't really "illegal," they are just "out of status."

"Founding Fathers" is now considered to be sexist. It is suggested that these men should now be referred to as "The Founders."

It is no longer considered appropriate to say that someone is "fat"; you have to pretend they are "weight challenged." Or we use cute little words like "chubby" or "pudgy." Or people will call themselves "big-boned." A woman recently wrote me an e-mail about my use of the word "fat" and told me that she wasn't fat at all but was actually big-boned. I informed her that was not true and that her bones were the same size as the bones of other people but that she had surrounded her poor bones with pounds and pounds of extra fat. I went on to add that dinosaurs had big bones, not her. As a result, she dropped me as her friend on Facebook. I'll miss her.

As an Okie I can relate to this one completely: "Trailer parks" are now "mobile home communities." By the way, "Okie" is considered by some to be a derogatory term thanks to Steinbeck's *The Grapes of Wrath*. I know my dad didn't like it. However, I'm pretty proud of it and it doesn't bother me. Neither does being called a redneck.

When people say "with all due respect," it's a PC way of saying, "I think you're an idiot and have no respect for you or what you just said." I would never use the words "with all due respect" and neither would anyone else who possessed a pair. A person who has a pair would just say, "I don't agree and here's why." But that means you must be willing to disagree and voice an opinion that states the other person is wrong. Most don't have enough of a pair to do that.

Now I know that some of these examples may seem extreme to you—and they are. But they are true examples of what is going on in our society. We use political correctness as a crutch to avoid straight talk. We have become so quick to take offense when we hear someone speak the truth that we do our best to water it down and dumb it down until we can barely discern what the original meaning was.

This has to stop! Just say it. If you are fat, you're fat. If you are broke, you're broke. If you talk too much, you aren't wordy; you need to shut the hell up because you have diarrhea of the mouth. If you are behaving like an idiot and someone calls you on it, they aren't mean; they're honest. If you say you are going to do something and then you don't do it, you are a liar. You can't dress it up and put a happy face on it, or call yourself "truth challenged"—you are a liar. Deal with it. It may not be kind, but it's still the truth. And we are sorely in need of more truth. In fact, I am one of those people that actually believes that telling the truth is kind.

Another biggie (remember, I warned you!):

PEOPLE WILL DO WHATEVER THEY CAN GET AWAY WITH.

This is probably the primary cause of the problems that we are facing today. And the problem with this problem is that it is just human nature. It's natural to push limits. It's who we are and what we do. Little kids will push every limit they come up against. They should. It's the only way they can learn what limits are and how to live within boundaries. If there are no boundaries, they never learn anything. If you are a parent, at least a responsible parent, you will establish limits and boundaries for your kids to push up against. That's *your* job. It's the same way with employees and students. People will do anything and everything they can until someone stops them from doing it and sets limits and imposes consequences. Therefore, the solution to this problem is to let people get away with less.

Stop tolerating stupidity and poor performance. Stop letting people get away with bad behavior. Break this natural cycle with yourself, with your family, and with your coworkers and employees. It won't change the world, but it just might change *your* world.

WE ARE A NEEDY BUNCH!

Have you noticed how needy we have become as a society? We have lost our independence. We have become so socially dependent that we need others in order to feel good about ourselves, and others to blame when we don't feel good about ourselves. We are needy in so many ways.

The need to blame others

"It's not my fault." If there were ever a way of thinking that ticks me off, it's this one. We have got to reach the point where we take responsibility for the things that are happening in our lives—good or bad.

Your thoughts, your words, and your actions created the life you are living. You create your results— no one else. If you are broke, you spend too much. If you are fat, you eat too much. If people don't like you, you're a jerk. If you got fired, you weren't working hard enough. Or as I am well known for saying, "If your life sucks, it's because you suck!" And even if we set all of that aside and say that something horrible just fell out of the sky and devastated your world, what you choose to do about that horrible thing that happened to you is still your fault.

Folks just can't accept that. They cling to the need to blame others. In fact, we are encouraged to blame others. Turn on the television and watch all of the accident lawyers tell you that you should sue. For what? Who cares? Just sue! The bankruptcy guys, along with the credit counselors, will tell you that your credit card problems are not your fault at all; it's the fault of those pesky credit card companies. They will tell you not to feel bad that you maxed out your card (in reality, probably several cards) and that they can stop those big, bad, mean credit card companies from calling you and trying to collect their money. Never mind that you signed a contract promising to pay them; that's not your fault either! Thousands of lawyers have made their careers based on this silliness. Their ads have cute little jingles that you can sing right now. That's how entrenched these bottom-feeders have become in our society.

Did you spill your coffee in your lap while you were driving because you found it just too difficult to drive, text, and drink coffee while shoving that Egg McMuffin down your throat? No problem! Again, that is not your fault! Just sue because the coffee was hot (you know, like they promised it would be) and you got burned because you were clumsy.

Oh yeah, and it's not your fault that you were texting on your cell phone and walked into a fountain at the mall. You get to sue because you were embarrassed. Yep, don't embarrass me for being a dumbass or I will sue you! After all, I can't be blamed for being a dumbass; it has to be someone's fault! It's the fault of the mall for putting that big fountain in the middle of the mall and it's the fault of the fountain builder, as well as the zoning commission for allowing the mall to be built in the first place.

In situations like these (true situations, by the way) people who have a pair would just say, "Damn, I'm clumsy!" and then clean themselves up and move on. Or if they started to complain too much, a friend with a pair would pull them aside and say, "Hey, dumbass, this was your own stupid fault. Stop whining, suck it up, grow a pair, and move on. You look like an idiot making a big thing out of this!"

But our society lets people get away with this silliness. We allow people to abdicate personal responsibility and blame others. The more blame you are allowed to place on others, the less blame you have to take yourself. Suddenly nothing is your fault because there is always someone else you can find to blame. All of this comes from a lack of personal responsibility. This creates an entitled society where people believe they are *owed* a living. When you become entitled, you abdicate the throne of personal responsibility and allow yourself to become someone else's responsibility. You don't have to step up and be responsible in an entitlement society. Your pair can just shrivel away as you wait on your handout.

The need for approval

I went shopping with my wife the other day. She went in the dressing room and tried on a dress. By the time she made it out of the changing room to the chair where I was waiting, three clerks had said to her, "That looks so cute on you!" I was watching them as they said it and one of them never even looked at her, so how did she know? And you know what? It didn't look cute on her. She knew it and I knew it. They knew it too, but they were more interested in the sale than in her looking cute, so they lied to her. Luckily my wife has a pair and trusts her own opinion and my opinion enough that a retail clerk being paid to hustle clothes won't sway her. But there are plenty of people who buy ugly clothes and end up looking like hell in them simply because some clerk told them they looked cute. This is sad and pitiful and based in a lack of confidence—and rooted in not having a pair.

The need to feel special and loved

How pitiful it is that people need constant reassurance that they are loved and that every word they say is brilliant and that everything they do is worthy of praise and flattery. I think that is why Facebook is so popular. You can post, "I woke up this morning," and fifty of your so-called friends will be right there to say, "Good for you! We knew you could do it! We missed you while you were asleep! We love you! Be sure to post what you had for breakfast so we can ooh and aah over that too!" Holy crap! You aren't special. Get that through your brain. Your parents lied to you. You were special to them, because they were your parents. It's your birthright to be special to your mama and daddy but the rest of us actually expect you to do something! We don't care one hoot about who you are; we only care what service you provide. If you aren't making a contribution to us, then you are in our way. Harsh? Yeah, probably, but it's reality.

Get over yourself and stop being so damn needy. People who have a pair live their lives without the constant need for validation or the brainless yammerings of their peer group. They are who they are and are fine with it whether anyone else likes it or not!

I like how Steven Pressfield put it in his great book, *Turning Pro*: "When we truly understand that the tribe doesn't give a damn, we're free. There is no tribe, and there never was. Our lives are entirely up to us."

The need to make everyone happy

The constant need to make everyone else happy at the cost of your own happiness will destroy you. I've seen people who live their lives for the sole purpose of making others happy, and ultimately they end up miserable and sad and lonely. Besides, you can't really make other people happy, so forget it. It can't be done. People are happy or unhappy all on their own and you have little to do with it. In fact, the last thing in the world I want is someone trying to happy me into happy. I hate that. Leave me alone and let me be the way I want to be. Give up the need to please others by sacrificing your own needs. My advice: Make yourself happy and surround yourself with people who are cool with that.

> I don't know the key to success,
> but the key to failure is trying to please everybody.
>
> —Bill Cosby

The need to compromise between right and wrong

I believe that things are either right or they are wrong. There is no in-between. Right should not be compromised.

Some of my readers have had their blood pressure soar about my black-and-white approach to self-improvement, finances, parenting, and life in general. They have pointed out that there are several areas in life that really are gray. No kidding. Thanks for pointing that out to me. I had no idea that was the case. How could I know that? I have never had a problem or faced a challenge. I have never raised teenagers, had money issues, been married or divorced, held a job, managed people, driven down the street, eaten out, bought anything, received a bill, or had to make a tough decision. Never. None of those things. I have lived a completely sheltered life in a cave, blessed with only positive thoughts and outcomes. I have never had to face all of the things real people face and I honestly had no idea that life had any gray areas.

Come on—I know life is full of gray areas. It's just that I think we have all become way too comfortable living in those gray areas. Gray areas used to be little tiny corners we could escape to in order to justify our stupid actions and results. Now the gray areas are everywhere: our homes, our businesses, our government, our society, our grocery stores, in our books, magazines, and newspapers, and all over our televisions. Our leaders spew gray and drape it in red, white, and blue. Things are so gray that when someone actually draws a line and paints one side black and the other side white, it bothers the hell out of people! We have become comfortable and have begun to embrace the gray areas way too much and to shy away from the uncomfortable realities of black and white. I want people to begin to think more in terms of black or white, right or wrong, good or bad. People need to understand they are either doing enough or they aren't doing enough. We need to recognize that we are either giving our best or we aren't. You are either on the way or you are in the way. You are either living within your means or you aren't. It's either the truth or it's a lie.

It's easier to live in the black-and-white world. That's why I am so confused by those who love the gray area. When faced with a decision, people who live in a black-and-white world just make it quickly based on whether it is the right thing to do or the wrong thing to do. You don't have to wallow in it, meditate on it, study it, consider it, hold a focus group, or take a vote. You *do* the right thing. Why? Because you can. All it takes is some guts. A backbone. A pair.

You will be criticized for it. Trust me, I know. Who cares? You will be given grief at work for kissing up by doing your job when others are slacking. Tell them to kiss off. Your friends will give you crap about being too tough on your kids. They will laugh at you for saying no to spending money when you know you can't afford it. They will ridicule you for not taking the easy road when you know you should take the right road. Those people are not your friends, so dump them. Now. And never look back.

Do the right thing in your life every time, to the best of your ability. You won't be perfect at it. I'm certainly not. I mess up every day and slip and slide around in the gray area, just like everyone else. But every day, I remind myself I can do a little better: I can take a stronger stand for what I know is right and I can take action on it. That's all it takes: a decision to do it, a willingness to take action, the humility to admit you aren't doing your best, the honesty to confront yourself for it, and the willingness to keep on doing what you know is right regardless of the consequences. Yep, that's it: It's black or white.

If it's right and no one else is doing it, it's still right.

If it's wrong and everyone else is doing it, it's still wrong.

The need to avoid conflict
Some people avoid conflict like the plague, and I believe it's for two reasons:

1. They are ill equipped for the fight.

    This one can actually be a strength if you understand it. If you don't know what you are talking about, don't open your mouth pretending you do and prove you are an idiot. I was a guest on *Bulls & Bears* on Fox Business one day, talking about some facet of the economy, and they asked me a question that I was honestly clueless about. I answered, "I don't have a clue." They said, "Really, Larry?" I said, "Yep, not a clue. In fact, I don't even know what you're talking about." One of the hosts laughingly said, "No one ever admits that on television, Larry." I said, "Well, they ought to; that way they wouldn't end up looking stupid after they said it." I got a lot of great feedback from that exchange. People too often speak without knowing what they are talking about. Then they make themselves look ridiculous. When you point that out to them, they get pissed that you made them look stupid. Seems they are clueless that they made themselves look stupid with their uninformed, ignorant opinion. I get into these arguments a lot on Facebook when I post a controversial statement. People jump all over me to argue and while I love a good argument, some of these good folks are just so ignorant of the facts that they really should keep their mouths shut. But they don't.

As I often tell them when they argue with me, "You have made the mistake of coming to a gunfight armed with only a rubber knife."

2. They are genuinely afraid they will get hurt.

   Yeah, it happens. Anytime you go into battle, either verbally, physically, or in a business negotiation, there is a chance you will lose. The truth is that sometimes you get your ass kicked. No matter what you have done to prepare, it happens. You don't always win, and to expect to always win is naïve. But if you don't stand up for yourself and at least get into the battle, you will never even have the chance of winning. Remember the words of Shane Falco (Keanu Reeves) in *The Replacements*: "Pain heals. Chicks dig scars. Glory lasts forever."

The need to appear perfect

We have this idea that if people see our flaws then they won't respect us. Nothing could be further from the truth. In all of my books, I have exposed my flaws. I take responsibility for them, admit them openly, and discuss what I learned from my mistakes. In my book *People Are Idiots and I Can Prove It!*, I even wrote a section called "Larry Winget: Idiot Extraordinaire," where I laid out every stupid thing I could think of, from my failures in business to my failures as a husband, a parent, and as a person. I have found that people are very forgiving and accepting of anyone who admits their mistakes and takes responsibility for them. It's when we don't admit our mistakes and pretend to everyone that we are perfect that we get in trouble. Each of us can think of dozens of examples of this with our politicians and other celebrities. I know I have said many times, "If they would just admit it, own it, and apologize for it, I would forgive them!"

The need to avoid criticism

Our fragile little selves just can't stand to have anyone criticize us these days. "Don't you dare tell me I'm not good at something—you might hurt my feelings." Well, to hell with your feelings. If you are a screwup, you need to hear that you are a screwup so you will stop being one. If it hurts your feelings, good. Your feelings don't matter when your results suck. You need to get better. So stop your whimpering and take your criticism. Criticism is how we grow. If you heard "great job" every time you attempted something, you wouldn't improve much, would you? So accept the criticism. Even welcome it. Take it like a man—even if you're a woman!

When I was a kid, if you failed to learn a subject in school, you failed. Somewhere along the way we got so soft we didn't think that a kid's fragile psyche could handle hearing that he failed at something, so we started using words like "needs improvement." Needs improvement? Hell yes, he needs improvement—he failed; he needs a lot of improvement! We need to teach our kids to take failure and learn from it and behave differently so it doesn't happen again. Does that happen? No. Instead, we protect our kids from words like "failure" so they never have to confront their failings. Then they grow up and enter the workforce and can't handle it when their boss tells them that they are screwing up and alienating customers and costing the business money. And subsequently they get fired. Wouldn't we serve our kids better if we got them used to the idea of failure and how to overcome it early on, instead of waiting until they have rent and car payments and others depending on them?

WHAT DOES HAVING A PAIR LOOK LIKE?

Okay, we all know what an actual pair looks like but I want you to think about what it looks like to have a pair. What attributes do these paired-up people possess that sets them apart from the masses?

History is full of people with a pair. In fact, these people made our country great. It took a pair for our Founding Fathers to stand up against the British and to form a new government in a new country. Abraham Lincoln was a politician with a pair. Margaret Thatcher was another.

Ronald Reagan certainly proved that he had a pair when he said, "Mr. Gorbachev, tear down this wall."

But there are many lesser-known politicians too. Edmund Ross, the senator who cast the deciding vote against the impeachment of President Andrew Johnson, for example. He knew it was going to cost him the senate seat he loved and in fact said that he was "looking down into my own open grave" before he voted to acquit. Can you think of a politician today who would stand by his principles in the face of losing his career?

Gandhi proved that you could be a pacifist and still have a pair.

We have military heroes that also certainly qualify. George Patton comes to mind immediately. Audie Murphy is another, not as a movie star, even though he made many movies, but as most decorated soldier of World War II—the Medal of Honor, the Bronze Star, and a Purple Heart just to name a few. But let's also look at people who weren't generals or who didn't become movie stars as a result of their service. Look at the enlisted men and women who serve us every day. The people this book is dedicated to. (Did you miss that? Go back and look at the dedication.) Look at the story of Marcus Luttrell, the Navy SEAL who was stuck behind enemy lines, and read his great book, *Lone Survivor*. Consider the men and women who are wounded and come back home only to face the incredible challenges of trying to live a normal life without a limb or worse. They don't whine, they don't complain; they face their issues and move on with more courage than I could ever muster. Think of all of those who serve us as police and firefighters. These are brave souls who put their lives on the line to make sure we get to live more safely.

In business, you have Fred Smith. In college, Fred wrote a paper about an overnight delivery service and while everyone told him that it wasn't feasible, he made it the reality that is Federal Express. And Tony Hsieh. Tony started with an online advertising network that later evolved into the online shoe retailer Zappos, which he sold to Amazon for $1.2 billion. And Mary Kay Ash, the founder of Mary Kay Cosmetics. Mary Kay was passed over for a promotion because she was a woman, and that inspired her to start a cosmetics company that allowed women to sell cosmetics door to door and become the designers of their own futures. Because of her, there are a lot of pink Cadillacs on the road today!

In sports, the first name that comes to mind is Jackie Robinson, who has to be the bravest man with the biggest pair in the history of sports. Babe Didrikson also immediately comes to mind, undoubtedly our finest female American athlete.

By the way, if any of these names don't ring a bell for you, then do yourself a favor and become familiar with each of them. Take a few minutes to at least Google these folks and make yourself aware of their remarkable achievements.

When considering names to include in this section of the book, I asked a handful of my buddies to tell me who came to mind for them when they thought of people in their lives who had a pair. My friend Joe Calloway from Nashville, author of the great book *Becoming a Category of One*, sent me this:

"The black kids who did the lunch counter sit-ins in the 60s in Nashville. And any little black kid who was the first or among the first to integrate a school. I remember being in the 7th grade and *one* little black boy walks into our opening day assembly in Junior High School. He was the very first black kid in our school. Kids and parents were booing. This little boy and his mom walked in, heads held high, and took their seats. I thought to myself, 'That's the bravest kid and mom I've ever seen.'"

There have been incredible people who have had a pair in entertainment as well. Elvis for being an original. Same for Little Richard. Being an original is tough in any business but these guys did it, were authentic, and changed music forever.

John Wayne had a pair like no other actor ever in every role he ever played. Clint Eastwood's Dirty Harry had a pair for sure. In fact, the movies are full of examples of people with a pair. That's why some movies become such big hits—not because the acting is great, but because the story has heart and the character, though many times very flawed, has a pair. We all admire that in a character and are attracted to them for that reason alone.

How about Rocky, an underdog who fought back and "took his shot" at being great? In this case you should even think of Sylvester Stallone, who wrote the screenplay and refused to sell it unless he got to star in it. And even though he was flat broke and desperate, he held out and his entire career was launched because he stayed true to what he believed in.

Liam Neeson's character in *Taken* is a great example of having a pair. He told his daughter's kidnappers exactly what he was going to do to them if they didn't let her go, and then he did exactly what he said he would do. He delivered on his word and because of it they felt the consequences of their actions.

One of my favorite examples of having a pair was Captain Woodrow Call in *Lonesome Dove*, a great book and probably the best thing ever put on film. Woodrow carried the dead body of his best friend, Gus, three thousand miles to bury him, simply because he gave his word that he would do it. That was a time when people took giving their word very seriously. I admire that.

My dad had a pair. He took guff from no one. When he was an eighteen-year-old serving in the navy during World War II as a first-class seaman, the ship's captain called him a son of a bitch and my dad punched him in the face for it. No man was allowed to call his mother a bitch. He was busted back to second-class seaman and avoided the brig because they were in the

middle of the Pacific fighting a war. He was the one who taught me that when you give your word, you keep it no matter what. A lot like Woodrow Call, I suppose. He taught me that a man is only as good as his word and he ingrained that into me from birth.

You know people who exemplify the attitude I am talking about in this book—probably not famous people but just good, regular folks. Folks who are in charge of their lives and stand up and fight back in the face of overwhelming odds. Maybe you know a single mom who doesn't play victim but is in control of her life and works hard to take care of her kids financially and as a parent. Or someone who served time in prison but ultimately took responsibility for their life and is now rehabilitated and contributing positively to society.

So, back to my original question: What does having a pair look like? You tell me. Here's what I want you to do: I want you to stop right now, get a pen, and make a list of people who, in your opinion, have a pair. Then I want you to write down next to their name what it is about them that causes you to admire them. If you honestly can't think of people in your life who have a pair, then make a list of the attributes that a strong, responsible, independent person embodies.

Name	Attribute
————————	————————
————————	————————
————————	————————
————————	————————
————————	————————
————————	————————
————————	————————
————————	————————
————————	————————
————————	————————
————————	————————
————————	————————

Now that you have filled out the list, consider how you can take this list of attributes you admire in these people and develop them in your own life.

Make another list:

Attribute I Admire	Plans for Developing It in My Life
———————	———————
———————	———————
———————	———————
———————	———————
———————	———————
———————	———————
———————	———————
———————	———————
———————	———————
———————	———————
———————	———————

This is an assignment that can change your life. It can change your business and every relationship you have. It will bring back sanity to your life. And if enough of us grow a pair by developing these types of attributes, we can take back our country and our world.

Interesting sidenote

You just established what having a pair looks like to you. I'm betting that these words didn't appear anywhere on your list:

Rude
Obnoxious
Loud
Arrogant
Self-centered
Mean
Discourteous
Overly aggressive
Intolerant

Yet to a good portion of the world, this list represents what it means to have a pair. Sad. I'm going to deal with this issue in a few pages but in the meantime, let's discuss how you go about growing a pair.

HOW DO YOU
GROW A PAIR?

I want the world to change. I want it to be full of people who take responsibility and do the right thing.
But that's not how it works. You can't just wave a wand
and have the world be a different place. You can't wish
for things to change and expect it to happen. The world
changes one person at a time. I learned that all on my
own, the hard way. I used to wish the world was a certain way but only ended up being disappointed. As a
business owner and supervisor, I worked with my employees on their performance, hoping they would
change. They didn't. Later, as I got into my current
profession, I gave speeches thinking people would listen to my words of common sense and decide to go be
different. For the most part, it didn't happen. I wrote
books like this one and I honestly believed that people
would read them and go out and act differently, thus
making the world a better place. Even when my books
hit the bestseller list, the world remained much the
same. I've worked with people one on one, coaching

them on television and in my office. Some of them changed but the world certainly didn't. So I gave up on changing the world. Instead, I decided to focus on changing myself. When I changed myself, the way I dealt with the world changed. When I grew a pair, the way the world is didn't bother me nearly as much because I was suddenly in control. I was not in control of *the* world (damn it!) but I was in control of *my* world.

I'm betting you want the world to change too. But since that isn't going to happen, you have to change yourself.

This is how you change yourself: a little at a time. I get sick of the motivational bozos telling you how easy it is to change your life. Buying into this is setting yourself up for failure. The truth is that it's hard to change your life. In reality, all you can do is change one little thing at a time. Then you change one more little thing. And eventually, when you have stacked enough of those little changes on top of each other, you end up with a life that looks different than the old one you were living. That's how you change yourself and your world. And when enough people do that, then you end up with a change in the world.

Before I give you some things you can do to grow a pair, I want to make something clear: *Anyone* can grow a pair.

Growing a pair is for everybody. It's not just for people like me. It's not just for big guys or CEOs and it's not just for female MMA fighters. This state of mind is appropriate for every type of person. It's good for every personality style. You can be as meek as a lamb and still have a good-size pair on you. My wife is the world's greatest peacemaker, with a kind word for everyone (yes, the exact opposite of me), and yet she has a huge pair. She knows how to stand up for herself and is always treated with respect. Why? Because she won't accept anything other than that. It is her state of mind. I can show you little kids in wheelchairs that get treated with respect because they have a pair. There are ninety-five-pound women you would never think about talking back to and it's all because of their attitude.

You don't have to be a loud person or a big person or an outgoing person. You have to get your mind right. When you get your mind right and the pair in place, the rest falls into place.

Now it seems that the only time people are willing to have a pair is after the fact. People are full of "what I should have said or done was . . ." News flash: It does no good to grow a pair after the event is over and done with. Growing a pair isn't an afterthought. It isn't something that allows you to look back with regret at what you should have or could have done. Living with a pair is proactive, not reactive.

GROW A PAIR—IT BEGINS WITH YOU!

Now that you understand what having a pair looks like and you know that you want to change your world, you've got to start by fixing yourself. Let's talk about specific things you can do—starting with you—to grow a pair.

Speak up!

You've heard me saying that a lot in this book already, but now it's time to get into the nitty-gritty of what that really means. It's simple. Let your thoughts be known.

When people say hurtful things to you, tell them you don't appreciate it. When you see someone who is clearly walking around just fine take a handicapped parking spot, say something to them and then report them. When people talk in theaters, tell them to be quiet.

> Never be bullied into silence. Never allow yourself to be made a victim. Accept no one's definition of your life; define yourself.
>
> —Harvey Fierstein

Let me give you an example of what I mean. I had just boarded an airplane one day and was nestling down into my seat. I fly first class because at this point in my life I am "Chairman," "Executive Platinum," and every other elite status that you can achieve on most airlines. It's what comes with twenty-plus years spent on airplanes. As the rest of the plane was boarding, a very loud, and I mean *very* loud, woman was walking down the aisle screaming into her cell phone. I turned and watched this woman in disbelief and could see she was in row thirty-five or so at the back, yet I could still hear every word of her side of the conversation. She then told the person she was talking to that they should call her back, and as she put her bags up and took her seat, she gave them her phone number so they could call. I pulled my cell phone out and dialed the number she had just announced to 150 people on a full airplane. When she answered, she said, "Who is this?" I said, "I'm a guy sitting up in first class in row three. You are thirty rows behind me and I can hear every word of your conversation. In fact, every person on this plane can hear every word of your conversation. Would you mind speaking a little more quietly when your friend calls you back?" She started screaming at me, saying things like "How dare you!" and "Well, I never!" She said, "Show yourself!" So I stood up, turned, and waved and smiled at her. She then suggested that I go do a lewd act with myself that I believe would be physically impossible. I laughed and sat back down. Was I rude? Some would say so. Personally I think that she was rude and I was just pointing it out to her. Others on the plane could hear the entire exchange and several shouted thank-yous to me when it was over. This may seem to be an extreme example to you but I seem to live an extreme life so this stuff really happens to me. While you probably won't find yourself in a situation like this, you will find yourself in a thousand smaller situations every week where either you or someone else is being taken advantage of.

A polite word spoken with conviction is a powerful tool. Try it.

And under this little heading of speak up: Speak up! That means don't mumble, don't whisper or be a "low talker," and don't rush through your words. Speak with a sense of purpose, as if what you have to say is worth listening to, and then do your best to make sure it is.

Stop using weak language.

Stop saying "I think" when you really know. If you know it, just say it. There is no need to preface your statements with "I think." We already know it's what you think because you are saying it. Besides, why do you only think it? Don't you know? "I think" is a statement of weakness. Stop thinking and start knowing.

Or even the more ridiculous "in my humble opinion." Why should your opinion be a humble opinion? If you have an opinion, just express it and be proud of it. If you aren't proud of it, then keep your mouth shut.

Or how about saying "excuse me" when you haven't interrupted or bumped into someone or sneezed or belched or passed gas. What are you being excused for? Existing?

"You know what I mean?" No, we don't know what you mean and obviously you don't either, you moron. Which is much like "you know what I'm saying?" Except in that case, I do know what you're saying. You are saying that you are too stupid to be in a conversation with!

Learn to speak well.

Use good grammar. Your point is completely under-mined when you say "I seen it" instead of "I saw it." The same goes for your writing. Know the difference be-tween "your" and "you're" and between "their," "they're," and "there." Use them correctly. You can't make an intel-ligent argument when you write and speak like a moron.

Get to the point!

Have you ever found yourself in a conversation with someone, wishing that you had a remote control that could fast-forward through their inane rambling? I spend most of my life wishing that. Get to the point. Most people couldn't make a point with an ice pick.

One of my favorite television scenes is James Gar-ner playing *Lonesome Dove*'s Captain Woodrow Call in *Streets of Laredo*. In the middle of a conversation with some fellows, he suddenly says, "I find this conversa-tion tedious. Good-bye." Then he rides off. Now that's having a pair!

Ask for what you want.

Don't assume that people know what you want. Don't assume that people can read your mind and can guess what you want. Don't expect that what you want will be magically attracted to you. *Ask!* Want a raise? Do the work, document your achievements, earn it, and then ask for it. When you want more, ask for more. Ask more from others and ask more of yourself.

Don't be anonymous.

If you're going to speak up and tell people what you think, then have a big enough pair to do it without the anonymity of the Internet. And if you must post a comment, have the cojones to own up to your opinion and use your real name! I encounter this problem a lot due to my online presence. I hate the spineless weasels who don't like what I have to say and instead of confronting me, they create a Facebook page with no picture in order to attack me anonymously. I've had death threats from Yahoo! and Gmail accounts that don't exist five minutes after the people tell me I need to die for taking some of the stands I do. None of these blustering fools would ever say any of the things they say on Facebook to my actual face. Why? They are cowards. They only know how to voice their strong opinions behind the veil of anonymity. Don't be that way ever! If you are going to say something bold, then grab your pair and look that person in the eye and get it said and take the consequences, whatever they might be. If you aren't willing to do that, then keep your mouth shut.

Stop apologizing

. . . for telling the truth.

I know as well as anyone that people hate hearing the truth. I take a lot of guff for telling the truth. So will you. Take the guff you will inevitably receive and move on. Remember, the truth doesn't care whether you like it or not. It's the truth.

. . . *for being who you are.*
Unless you're stupid. Or an asshole. In that case, don't apologize; just stop being a stupid asshole. Remember, it's better to be an authentic asshole than a fake sweetie pie!

. . . *for being.*
Stop apologizing for your thoughts by opening your statements with "I'm sorry, but . . ." What in the hell are you sorry for? For disagreeing? For speaking up? For having an opinion in the first place? Did you do something wrong? If you didn't, then stop saying you're sorry.

> Many people, especially ignorant people, want to punish you for speaking the truth, for being correct, for being you. Never apologize for being correct, or for being years ahead of your time. If you're right and you know it, speak your mind. Speak your mind. Even if you are a minority of one, the truth is still the truth.
>
> —Mahatma Gandhi

Become judgmental.
Judging is about taking a stand for yourself and for right and wrong. So cast off your inner weenie and start to judge people. And don't give me the "judge not,

that ye be not judged" crap. I am so sick of the holier-than-thou types telling me not to judge. I hate it when people start quoting the Bible to validate their own bad behavior. And those who love to use that verse tend to misinterpret the Bible and only tell half of the statement to make it work for them. The Bible actually says, "Judge not, that ye be not judged. For with what judgment ye judge, ye shall be judged: and with what measure ye mete, it shall be measured to you again." Therefore, if you are willing to be held to the same standard you hold others to, then get after it!

Besides, anyone who says they don't judge is a liar—either that or they are incredibly naïve. As an employer do you judge the actions of your employees? If you don't, then you aren't much of a leader or manager and your business will soon go out of business. As a parent do you judge the actions of your children? If your answer to that is no, you are a lousy parent. (I am going to address parenting with a pair and running your business with a pair later in this book.) How about the actions of your elected officials—do you judge them? These areas deserve a section all their own. Every time you vote you judge them. Do you not pick one store over another based on how you judge the quality of their merchandise, their service, and their prices? Those are all judgments. Do you not have the right to judge someone whose actions infringe on your rights, or cost you money, or someone who swerves into your lane of traffic? Of course you do. Laws are all based on judgments of the right and wrong of other people's actions. Without judgment, there would be chaos. I am not here to judge another person's value or worth—but their actions are a different story.

Success comes from what you do, not from what you say you are going to do.

Stop believing that it's all about you.

It isn't. That may surprise some of you more self-centered types. But I believe we would all be amazed at how little other people actually think about us at all. Yet we are all so sensitive these days that we think that everyone is picking on us. If I say that the majority of Americans are obese and use the statistics to support that statement, it is a generality that applies to our society. If you are obese, then you can take it personally if you want to but I don't know you and I am not writing about you personally. Stop letting your own guilt rule your reaction to a statement that was meant as a commentary on society.

I once told this joke from the stage at a convention where I was hired to speak: "What do an Oklahoma divorce and a tornado have in common? Either way, some ol' boy is going to lose his double-wide."

After the speech, when I was at the back of the room autographing books, a woman approached me, fuming with anger. She said, "I do not appreciate you making fun of fat women in your speech." I asked her to explain, as I knew that I hadn't done that or even come close to it. She said, "That joke about losing your double-wide." I explained to her that a double-wide meant a large mobile home, not a fat wife. But of course, she was big and fat and thought that I had singled her out and was making fun of her.

A woman even yelled at me after I told a story in one of my speeches using the word "lady." She told me that "lady" was a sexist term and she didn't appreciate being referred to as one. I told her that in her case, it was only because I hadn't met her yet.

Stop giving a damn.

Don't go crazy with this one. You should probably start giving a damn about a whole lot of things that in the past you haven't. Things like your financial situation, your work ethic, what your kids are learning, and your health. But there are just as many things that you should stop giving a damn about too. Like what others think of you. What others are going to say about you later. You can't control what others say or do so get past it. As long as you are saying and doing the right thing and being true to yourself, those you love, and what you believe, then it doesn't matter. Terry Cole-Whittaker wrote a great book many years ago entitled *What You Think of Me Is None of My Business*. Isn't that a great title? While there is little chance you will actually search out the book and read it, at least internalize the title.

What others think of you will have almost nothing to do with your success. I have been made fun of for years. I don't care. People make fun of my clothes and my jewelry and my accent. I can rarely walk down the street without them making comments about me because I do stand out in the crowd. You would think that after all of these years of looking different I wouldn't notice. I do. Every time, I notice. I just don't care. Besides, I secretly tell myself that they are saying that they would give anything to be able to dress like me!

Be honest.

Honesty is not the best policy; it's the *only* policy. If you want to be known as a person who has a pair, show up, tell the truth, and let go of the outcome.

Never make excuses.

People with a pair have reasons for things not working out; people without a pair have excuses for things not working out. People with a pair acknowledge the reason yet still take complete responsibility for the result. They don't bother with blame, and accept that regardless of what happened or didn't happen, the results are theirs and theirs alone. If they are late, while the traffic may have played a part and is the reason for them being late, they don't whine and blame; they simply take responsibility for being late, apologize, and move on.

When they can't pay their bills, they don't blame the credit card companies or predatory lenders or anyone else for their problem. Instead, they do what it takes to make the situation right. When they don't get their assignment done, they realize that regardless of the reason, it's ultimately their fault.

> He that is good for making excuses
> is seldom good for anything else.
>
> —Benjamin Franklin

Don't whine.
You have problems. I have problems. Everyone has problems. Big deal. Find me someone who doesn't. The only people who don't have problems are dead. I don't want to hear about yours and you don't want to hear about mine. Stop "sharing," tweeting, and posting on Facebook every ridiculous little bit of crap that happens to you. No one cares. They say they do, but they don't—I promise.

Walk away.
Become willing to walk away from people, situations, jobs, organizations, groups, and relationships that don't move you closer to your goals.

> You can't step up to the next level as long
> as you keep one foot on the lower level.

Become less tolerant.

I know this flies in the face of most of the PC crap we have been taught. You should be tolerant of who people are, but intolerant of their stupid actions.

Recently a hockey coach for a group of kids tripped a thirteen-year-old during the handshaking the kids do at the end of the game. The coach stuck his foot out and tripped the kid and the kid fell and broke his wrist. I found his actions so despicable that I just could not be quiet about it. Like thousands of others, I posted the video on Facebook and did my best to let people know what a deplorable human being I found this guy to be. I got a lot of support for my posting as so many found his horrible conduct unacceptable. Jim Bouchard, the author of *Think Like a Black Belt*, posted this comment:

"The proper response to incivility is not passivity or tolerance. This is why sharing this type of behavior is important. It's important that we don't escalate the incivility, but rather respond with demands for swift, firm and decisive action. Only when we're willing to take this type of action consistently—and be willing to stand firm when challenged—will we start to reverse this incredibly disgusting trend in our society."

Let's be clear here though. This is not an excuse to be anything but courteous. There is no reason to be crude or mean or antagonistic once you have grown your pair. Just speak up for yourself and others in a nice way.

I won't be wronged, I won't be insulted, and I won't be
laid a hand on. I don't do these things to other people and
I require the same from them.
                    —John Wayne as J. B. Books in *The Shootist*

Know when to draw the line and where to draw the line.

When what you want to do infringes on the rights of
another, draw a line and stay on your side of it. When
someone infringes on your rights, draw a line and don't
allow them to cross it.

Stop trying to make everyone else happy.

In fact, a guaranteed way to be miserable is trying to
make everyone else happy. Happiness is a personal
choice. If someone doesn't want to be happy, leave them
alone. You can't happy someone else into happy!

Become totally self-reliant.

People who have a pair don't rely on the government to
support them. They don't "occupy" or complain about
others having too much and they don't complain about
themselves having too little. They understand that
they are responsible for their own lives and that it is up
to them to make sure they have taken the appropriate
steps to take care of themselves.

Be decisive.

That means you have to choose. You can't have it all regardless of what the motivational bozos have told you. Saying yes to one thing means saying no to something else. Being decisive and choosing one thing over another means you are going to disappoint someone else. Get it straight that regardless of what you choose someone is always going to be disappointed in your choice. Big deal.

I see the public opinion polls and the political polls. It always seems like about 4 percent are undecided. I don't understand the term "undecided." How can you not know where you stand about an issue or about a candidate or about much of anything? How?

I was at a social function recently and someone brought up the topic of abortion rights and one guy said, "I don't really have an opinion about that." I said, "Really? You don't have an opinion about that? How can anyone who draws a breath not have an opinion about that?" What he really meant was, "I don't have the balls to express my opinion about that because if I do, someone might disagree with me and I would be forced to defend my position." In other words, "I'm a coward."

Of course, I don't understand people who go into a restaurant, look at the menu for twenty minutes, and then say to the waiter, "I can't really decide; what would you suggest?" Now I am all for asking servers what is really good today or for suggestions, but it's because I

want to know what's really good that day, never because I can't decide.

Make big, bold, brash, ballsy plans.

That's right—make a plan and write it down. Few people do this. Then they wonder why their life sucks. It's because they don't have a concrete plan to avoid the "suckage." They are just waiting for the next thing to happen to them so they can react to it. This is beyond stupid. Grow a pair and get in control.

> No one ever wrote down a plan to be fat, broke, stupid, lazy, unhappy, and mediocre. Those are the things that happen to you when you don't have a plan.

Do the right thing.

And you never have to ask if something is the right thing. You know! And remember: If it's right and no one else is doing it, it's still right. If it's wrong and everyone else is doing it, it's still wrong.

That means you don't park in a handicapped parking spot with the excuse of "I'll only be a minute." That means you take the time to park between the lines so you don't take up two spots and inconvenience others. That means you hold the door open for others, even when it costs you a couple of seconds. That means you don't cut in line. That means you don't litter. That means you have your deposit ready before you are at the teller's window at the drive-in bank. That means in everything you do, you do the right thing—not the convenient thing for you, but the right thing for the greater good of all. Base your actions in courtesy and respect for other people, their time, and their property.

Don't allow people to take advantage of you.

Without exception, no one has the right to treat you badly, so stop giving them that right. We teach people how to treat us. If people are treating you badly, it is because you have allowed it. Stop allowing it.

Years ago, when I first became a professional speaker, I was hired to speak for a large state association. The opening speaker was their local congressman, who was a former television star and whose grandfather was one of the original founders of the association. He was to do forty-five minutes and then I was to go on and do forty-five minutes. The good congressman did his full time and was well on his way to blowing through all of my time when I told the meeting planner that it didn't look like I was going to go on. He said, "You're right; you probably aren't going on." I said, "That's okay. I'll just take my check and go home." He said, "No, we pay our speakers to speak and since you aren't speaking, we aren't going to pay. We paid for your flight, your meals, and your hotel—that's it." I said, "But it's your fault I'm not speaking because you didn't get the congressman off the stage." He said that's the way it goes, and turned to walk away from me. This was early in my career and I needed the money and I needed the referral to help me get more business. I didn't want to piss this guy off but I knew that pushing me around wasn't right. So I walked up on the stage and said, "Excuse me, congressman. I apologize and you are doing great up here and everyone wants you to continue. I just want to say one thing and then I'll let you have it back. That guy over there says I don't get paid unless I speak. So here you go—I'm speaking. Thanks and back to you, congressman." Then I walked over to the asshole meeting planner and said, "There. I spoke. I'll need my check now." He pulled it out of his pocket and I walked out of the room.

Don't brag.

If you have a pair, you don't have to brag about it; it will show in everything you say and do and even in how you carry yourself. People with a pair can "take" a room. I have seen people with that kind of charisma. I was in a burger joint in Tulsa one time when Oral Roberts, the famous televangelist, walked in and the entire energy in the restaurant changed. Whether you were a fan of his or not, you had to recognize that the man lived boldly and could take a room with his charisma.

Don't gossip.

Don't talk behind someone's back. If you don't have the balls to say it to their face, then keep your mouth shut. I know that would cut down on about half of people's conversations but think how much more pleasant the world would be.

**Look people in the eye
and have a good handshake.**

Much of that critical first impression we establish with people is based on these two things. Yet many people are terrible at this basic area of communications. I am always amazed when people look down at their feet and stick out their paw like it's a dead fish for me to grab and figure out what to do with it. Women have a tendency to present just their fingers for a handshake and I'm often left wondering whether I should kiss them as if she were the queen. When I see someone present just their fingers, I usually use just my fingers and shake theirs, making a joke out of it, and then say, "Now how about a real handshake?" Either that or I go ahead and awkwardly grab their fingers in an attempt to have a real handshake and internally write them off as a weak, submissive person or a conniving weasel. You may say that's an unfair judgment on my part but that doesn't matter, as it's too late; the judgment has already been made. So when it's time to shake hands, grab the hand firmly without causing pain and give it two or three shakes. Do this while looking the other person directly in the eyes. This shows you are confident and self-assured. Remember: People who have a *pair* need to have a *grip*.

Carry yourself like you have a pair.

Stand up straight. Hold your head high with your chin out. Walk like you are going someplace.

Have you ever been trying to get through the mall or down the street or through a door and there are people in the way who are just ambling? No sense of purpose, not going anywhere, just walking along like a goose waddling out of the water. You see it every day. So do I. Drives me crazy! Don't these people have some place to be? Even if they are window-shopping with nothing in the world on the calendar, they should walk like they have a sense of purpose.

How about employees? You walk in a store and the employee sees you but just can't make a move to walk toward you, and if they do, they look like they are on a casual stroll. Nearly every day of my young life my dad would say, "Step lively!" While I hated hearing it, it was great advice. I learned to indeed step lively in all that I did. It has served me well professionally as people know I have a sense of urgency when I am called or needed. If you have ever played on a team, you've heard the coach shout, "Hustle!" When you heard it, you hustled. You picked up the pace. You ran a little faster and a little harder. You increased your effort. When I walk into a store and a clerk approaches to help me, it's all I can do not to yell, "Hustle! Step lively!"

Be prepared.

I have written in my books, "Expect the best, but be prepared for the worst." While most of us are pretty good at expecting the best, very few do anything to prepare for the worst. This is evidenced by people's savings accounts! But I think it's time to take preparation to the next level. Therefore, I have become a prepper. No, I am not one of those wacko survivalists you see on YouTube, not by any stretch of the imagination. And don't expect to see me as a featured extremist on the next season of *Doomsday Preppers*. I am a realist and I don't want to find myself unprepared. I enjoy being in control of my situation as best I can. The facts are pretty clear: Our economic system worldwide is a disaster. The USA is so upside down on its debt, with no solution at hand to fix any of it, that I am not seeing a good way out of our mess right now. I don't think our entitled citizenry is above revolting like we have seen in France, Greece, and the UK. Natural disasters are increasing, causing power outages and other issues that either force people to leave their homes or force people to stay in their homes. A recent report by the government said that our power grids are particularly susceptible to hackers. Our borders are weak and our enemies are strong and sneaky. There are many people and nations who simply don't like us and wish us harm—including many individuals right here in our own country. We are vulnerable on many levels. Even FEMA suggests that every person store at least three days' worth of food and water in case of an emergency. Our grocery stores do not carry enough food to last three days if they lose power. So what happens to you and your family if your area loses power for a week, or even a day? Or if a natural disaster hits your area? Or if there is a revolt due to economic collapse? Are you prepared?

If you live in a climate where there is snow, you know you should put a blanket and some sand and other supplies in your car in case you get stuck. You probably carry a jack and a spare tire and jumper cables in your car "just in case." Yet that is most people's entire level of preparedness. Most people don't have enough food in their homes to make dinner. If every fast-food restaurant in their neighborhood closed, they wouldn't even be able to have dinner tonight. That's dumb, naïve, and irresponsible. I have food and water put away to last my family for a full year. It's easy to do and not much money and actually a fun family activity. I have a generator and plenty of gas to keep it running for months. I can cook even if all power is gone. I can defend my family and my property if needed. I am prepared in every way I can think of, not out of fear but because I am smart and have taken the time, the energy, and the small investment it takes to care for my family "just in case." You may think this makes me a crazy survivalist; I think it just makes me a responsible person. And while I hope none of us ever has to be tested in this regard, I won't be one of those guys who looks back in regret because I couldn't be bothered with it or was afraid of how it looked or sounded to others.

Most people never expect anything bad to ever happen to them until it already has.

Say NO more.

Do you have things that you absolutely hate to do but still find yourself doing? Why? Stop doing them. In my life, I finally grew a pair with my wife and myself and made it clear that I would never eat with people I don't like. Sharing food with someone is an almost sacred event to me. I love food and I love eating it. I love the social part of sharing a meal. And I don't like to share a meal with people I don't enjoy. I may get sucked into many situations with people I don't like, but sharing a meal won't be one of them. I say no. Is this difficult? For my wife it is. She is the one who has to turn down the social invitations to go out for dinner. But for me, it's been one of the most freeing decisions I have ever made.

We are way too agreeable. We don't want to offend anyone by telling them the truth, so we agree to do just about everything we are asked to do. Then we hate ourselves for agreeing and resent them for asking. Instead, when you are asked to do something you don't want to do, just say no. If you feel compelled to explain why you are saying no, you can just tell the truth and say you don't want to. Or you can tell them that you choose to spend your time doing something else. Or you could just remember that you don't owe anyone an explanation and move on. Yes, some will think you are selfish. Good. Be selfish. Give yourself permission to be selfish with your time. After all, it is *your* time! You have every right to spend your time doing things that please you. Put your family and yourself and your happiness ahead of others—it's perfectly fine. Don't let others dictate your time by inflicting their guilt on you when you choose not to participate in their project.

Continue to learn.

You are more powerful and more confident when you are better informed. Face it: You aren't as smart as you need to be or pretend to be. Keep learning. Read. Watch educational television. (*The Bachelorette, The Real Housewives,* and *Here Comes Honey Boo Boo* aren't educational!) Spend your time getting more information so you will make more informed decisions and operate from a position of knowledge.

If you knew better, you would do better.

—Jim Rohn

Apologize.

I know that earlier I told you to stop apologizing and now I am telling you to apologize. So why the change of heart? There isn't a change of heart at all. Stop apologizing when you have done nothing wrong, but know that you should apologize when you actually have done something wrong. People who have a pair can admit when they are wrong. And believe it or not, like it or not, you really are sometimes wrong. In fact, a major part of learning to grow a pair is realizing just how imperfect you are, admitting your own stupidity, and acknowledging that you make plenty of mistakes. Making mistakes does have a negative impact on those we do business with, those we call friends, and our family. Ask forgiveness when you need to. That's not a sign of weakness but a sign of strength.

Be a pitbull.

I am the trademarked Pitbull of Personal Development®. I got that name because, like a pitbull, when I grab onto something I never let go. In fact, if a pitbull bites down on you, you will typically have to kill it before it will let you go. That's me. I find something I believe in and I don't let go. You would have to kill me before I would stop believing in truth, honesty, hard work, integrity, service to others, and the other principles I hold dear. What do you believe in? Do you believe in it enough to fight for it? To hang on in the face of challenge or danger? Are you a pitbull or a poodle? Become a pitbull.

Have clear priorities.

People don't live the life they dream of because it isn't important enough for them to do what it takes to live that kind of life. It isn't a priority. Priorities determine your actions and your actions determine your results. For instance:

If being financially secure is your priority, then you will do what it takes to be financially secure. On the other hand, if looking cute is important to you, then you will spend your money at the mall.

If your kids are your top priority, then you won't smoke, eat like a pig, be financially out of control, or be too busy to spend time with them.

If getting ahead at work is important to you, then you will show up early, stay late, and do more than you are paid to do.

If being healthy is important to you, then you will make it a priority and eat healthily and exercise.

See how it works? Your actions determine your priorities.

How do you know what your priorities are? Simple: Track your actions. Track your time. Track where you put all of your energy. Track your money. Your words will lie but your actions tell you the absolute truth every time.

Your time, energy, and money always go
to what's important to you.

Be clear about what you own and what owns you.

While you are tracking your time, track the amount of time you spend on your smartphone, iPad, computer, iPod, or other gadget. Do you own these things or do they own you?

How about Facebook? Twitter? Do they control your life? Do they control your relationships? How many times have you seen people out for dinner who can't even put down their damn phone long enough to eat, let alone enjoy their meal? Their imaginary friends on Facebook get more of their time and focus than the real friend sitting right across the table from them. I have a friend who invites us to dinner at his house with his wife, then texts his other friends during dinner with us. He can't put his phone down long enough to focus on us. Of course, I have enough of a pair to tell him that it's rude and that stops him for a while, but it makes me feel like the other conversations must be more interesting than the conversation we are having and I know that can't be true!

People can't even drive anymore without tweeting

and texting and e-mailing on their smartphones. People are being killed every day in automobile accidents because of this. Smartphones owned by stupid people.

I recently saw a tweet from a mother named Ellen that said, "I would probably pay more attention to my kids if they were on Twitter." Twitter is more important to her than her children. And she seems to be proudly flaunting her bad parenting on social media for all of her friends to see. I'm not her friend but I saw it and so did tens of thousands of other people. She probably thought that this posting was funny. Do you find it funny? I don't. Put down the damn phone and go talk to your kids. Face to face. Show them that they are more important to you than your Twitter feed.

How about your stuff? Does your stuff own you or do you own your stuff? I wrote a lot about this in my book *You're Broke Because You Want to Be.* I told my own story about how my Porsche went from being a symbol of my prosperity to a symbol of my stupidity. A beautiful Porsche that sat in my garage for two full years and I only drove it seven hundred miles in that entire time. It went through two batteries and a set of tires because of the heat in my garage and I never even took the time to enjoy this amazing car. The car, and the feeling it gave me as a possession, owned me; I clearly didn't own it. Yeah, my name was on the title, but that was about it.

I am going through the same thing right now with my house. I have done well in my life. I worked my ass off to go from broke and then bankrupt to a place I am very proud of. I live in a beautiful house. A huge, beautiful house. It has been featured twice on television, in *The Arizona Republic* newspaper, and on the cover and in a feature article of *Phoenix Home & Garden.* It's gorgeous. I am very proud of it. It is on one and a half acres of manicured perfection. It takes me, my wife, and an army of workers to keep it all looking great. And my wife and I live in about one-third of the house. That's dumb. At some point, it's not about being able to afford something; it's about whether it makes sense for your lifestyle and is in alignment with your priorities. So my wife and I are selling our house. We are downsizing to a house where we will live in the entire house. We are tired of spending our time maintaining a house that impresses others but takes too much time, energy, and money to do it. We have nothing to prove to others or to ourselves. We are tired of our house owning us instead of us owning it. So in this case, we grew a pair and are selling it.

Examine your own life. Among your possessions, what owns you? Is it your car? Your house? Your motorcycle or boat? Think about your time. Do you spend more time on the computer or on social media than you do on your health, with your family, or in your business? Even examine your hobbies and think about whether they own you. Take a good hard look at every aspect of your life and decide now whether you need to grow a pair and put things in their proper place.

Don't compromise your principles.

Principles are those simple truths that your life is based on. These principles govern your personal behavior and are the very foundation of your existence. So the first thing you need to do is define your principles. What are they?

Write down your top five life principles that you will never compromise:

1. _____

_____

2. _____

_____

3. _____

_____

4. _____

_____

5. _____

_____

Bet you found this to be harder than you thought it would be. Most people have never taken the time to identify the principles by which they live their life. Mine are honesty, responsibility, integrity, hard work, and authenticity. I won't be lied to and I won't lie. I take responsibility for my mistakes and I require that of others. I will stay true to myself and what I believe, whether others like it or not. And I will work as long as it takes and as hard as it takes to accomplish what I want to get done.

These are the things I will not compromise. There are others, but these are my big five.

I have a story about Sonic Drive-Ins that I often use when speaking. I love a good cheeseburger and onion rings and Sonic does a great job. The story goes that one day I drove in and they were having a special that included a Pepsi promotion. I hate Pepsi—I'm a Coke guy. It's a funny story about an exchange with the guy at Sonic over that Pepsi, and it has always been one of my popular stories. I was later hired by a big company to speak, and right before I went on stage, they told me that Pepsi was their sponsor and that my Sonic story was a problem. I told them that was fine: I just wouldn't tell the story. They told me that they loved the story and wanted the story to be included but that I should change it from "I hate Pepsi" to "I hate Coke." I said, "But I don't hate Coke. I love Coke. It's Pepsi I hate. And since they are the sponsor, I won't show any disrespect and will just do a different story." They asked me to reconsider just this one time for them and reminded me that they were paying me. I told them I wouldn't lie and I wouldn't change the story. I would leave the story out. I explained that it wasn't the story that was important and it wasn't about me liking Pepsi or Coke. It was a matter of integrity and I wouldn't compromise mine over something that didn't matter anyway. They didn't get it and weren't happy about it. And while that might sound like I made a big deal out of nothing and you might ask, "What could it hurt to change the story?" just know that is how corruption of one's integrity begins: one little slip at a time.

Don't compromise your principles for a job, not for the approval of others, and not for money. If you do, you will have a hard time forgiving yourself. You will know you have prostituted the core foundation of your existence for the temporary approval of some schmuck who doesn't give a crap about you, or for a few bucks. And you will be sorry. In the end, what you believe in is about all you've got. Stay true to those things.

Live your life by this code:

LARRY'S NUMBER ONE RULE FOR LIFE AND BUSINESS:

Do what you said you would do, when you said you would do it, the way you said you would do it.

This is all anyone wants from you. Your customers want you to do what you said you would do, when you said you would do it, the way you said you would do it. So does your boss. So does your spouse. So do your kids. By the way, this is all you want from the people you do business with too. It's what you want from your kids and from your boss as well. This one line can become the key to a great life of success, happiness, and prosperity. Live it in all that you do.

GROW A PAIR WITH YOUR MONEY

GET CONTROL OF YOUR MONEY!

Think you can have a pair and be out of control with your finances? It doesn't work that way. If your finances are out of control, it is proof that you lack discipline either with yourself or with someone in your family. People who have a pair know not to spend more money than they earn. They save, invest, and live within their budget. They have fiscal discipline. They pay their bills on time. They have a commitment to their commitments! They also don't let their spouse or kids put the family at financial risk by spending more than they should. People who allow this are called enablers. They enable others by allowing them to get by with bad behavior. Enablers don't have a pair.

People who have a pair are in control of their lives. They exercise personal responsibility and self-discipline. That means that they don't let another person or a habit, like spending, control their lives. If you spend more than you earn, you're an idiot. You have put your spending habits in charge of your life and that's just stupid. You have given up your power (your pair) to the momentary thrill you get from spending money. Does that even make sense to you? To me it doesn't. Grow a pair and get in control of your life, which includes your spending.

PAIRLESS EXCUSES ABOUT MONEY

If there's ever an area of life where people just can't stop making excuses, it's the area of money.

"I really need that!"

No, you don't. You want it. Understand the difference between a need and a want. Besides, sometimes it's about more than just need versus want. If you're broke, need and want have little to do with it. If you're broke, you need to think in terms of "can't live without it." You can talk yourself into thinking a want is a need, but sometimes you have to be strong enough to tell yourself the truth and the truth is that you can live without it. When you can tell yourself the truth and just walk away from spending money you don't need to spend in favor of saving it for another time, that's having a pair.

"I grew up poor."

People use their past to justify all kinds of things. They use growing up not having much as a reason they still don't have much. They use the idea that because they were poor their parents didn't teach them good money habits. Both of those points might be completely true but at a certain point you have to grow a pair and stop using your past as an excuse. Your past has passed. Stand up to it, look it clearly in the eye, and know that your past has no control over you. That's having a pair!

"I'm just too busy to earn more money."

I laugh when someone tells me how busy they are. Some of you are saying right now to yourself, "You wouldn't laugh if I told you how busy I am, Larry. I'm really busy!" Yeah, I would probably still laugh. I don't care how busy you are, you aren't as busy as you think you are. The average American spends thirty-two hours per month surfing the Internet for personal purposes. Surely some of that time could be recouped and spent in a more productive way. And let me stop you here before you start telling me how much you need to surf the Internet. I love surfing the Internet too. I learn a lot on the Internet as well. But I wouldn't let the Internet stand in the way of me earning more money for my family. The Internet is just one example of how we let our time get away from us and how we convince ourselves that we are just too busy to get more done. Track your time, telling yourself the

God's Honest Truth, and see how busy you *really* are. My bet is that you aren't as busy as you think you are and that there is plenty of time to do more work to earn more money. There might even be more time to enjoy your life and your family if you will just stop wasting the time you have.

"We're in a recession, Larry. Haven't you heard?"

Yeah, I think I read about that. I think it affected me a bit as well. Interesting that some people used the recession as an excuse to fail and some used it as an excuse to reinvent themselves, get stronger, work harder, serve their customers better, and grow their businesses. We all went through the same recession, yet some of us used it one way and some of us used it another. Some had a pair and some didn't. People with a pair look at things differently because they understand that they are in charge of their lives.

Here's what you need to know when it comes to money: You don't have a money problem. I know it may seem like you do but you don't. You have a thinking problem. You have an attitude problem. You have a self-esteem problem. You are lazy. You don't take responsibility. You lack goals. Your priorities are out of whack. In other words, you don't have a pair. Grow a pair and get control of your money!

PEOPLE WITH A PAIR CARRY CASH.

I have always had the philosophy "Carry heavy. Live light." In other words, have a pocketful of money, yet don't burden yourself with stupid spending and unnecessary stuff. I always carry a pocketful of cash. It gives me a certain sense of satisfaction and reminds me of when I was broke and didn't have any cash to carry, which reminds me of what I've done not to be in that situation. It's empowering. I am always amazed at the number of people who have no money on them. I mean none. They brag that they have a platinum credit card or a "titanium" card, so why would they need cash? Seriously? That's just a stupid argument. When I speak at events, I usually offer my books or DVDs or CDs at the back of the room for attendees to purchase. Invariably, there will be any number of people who are trying to write me a check or give me a credit card for a simple twenty-dollar transaction. Since I am often pressed for time at an event like this, I often only take cash to make things go faster. Some guy will always say, "I don't carry any money. My wife carries my money." I usually respond with, "Does she carry your pair too? You're a grown man and you don't have even twenty dollars in your pocket? Be a man and go get twenty bucks and come back and see me." I lose some sales that way but I don't care. A man (or woman) needs to have some cash in his pocket!

BEWARE OF OTHERS WHO ARE TRYING TO GET YOUR MONEY.

That's right: Beware. Whether you want to believe it or not, there are bad people out there whose goal is to do you harm. Their goal is to scam you and take your money. Not everyone wants the best for you. This is especially true during a recession. When times are tough, people are more susceptible to being taken advantage of and are more willing to turn their hard-earned dollars over to someone who makes big promises. This is not paranoia; this is reality. A heightened sense of awareness of your surroundings, your security, and your safety is important. You owe it to yourself and to your family to beware. Don't be so trusting that you end up being taken advantage of by the "users" in this world. And these "users" are not always bad guys with masks; some users appear to be the good guys. Some of these users have slick websites and promise you big incomes by buying into their systems. They tell you that if you will just send them money—usually way more money than you have—they can teach you how to use your expertise to write a bestselling book and to sell your knowledge to others. They promise that you can get rich by listening to them. They use "millionaire" or "seven-figure income" in their promises because they know that these words are emotional triggers that will make you sit up and pay attention. Everyone wants to be a millionaire and these charlatans promise to help you become one. Some promise you that your life will take a turn for the better if you will just come ride around with them in their Rolls-Royce for an hour for a few thousand bucks. These guys should be ashamed of themselves. These people are wolves in sheep's clothing, as the old saying goes. They have nothing to offer you. They sucker people every day with their slick words and big promises. Pay attention folks: It's hard to get rich. It takes work to become a millionaire. There is no easy way to do it. Very few people will ever achieve the kind of success these bozos offer to sell you. The numbers simply aren't in your favor. Don't waste your money or your time. Beware!

Principles for Growing a Pair with Money

It's time for another list. I have already asked you to come up with the principles that you are unwilling to compromise when it comes to living your life. You need principles for use of your money as well. Principles that, regardless of how little you have or how much you have, you will not compromise. List those five principles here:

1. _____

_____

2. _____

_____

3. _____

_____

4. _____

_____

5. _____

_____

GROW A PAIR IN BUSINESS

Now it's time to take your pair to work. You are going to need to use the same pair that you have been using in your personal life and at home, but now it has to get a bit bigger to encompass you in the workplace among your coworkers, your employees, your employer, and your customers.

WORK

People who have a pair do all they are paid to do and then some. Give a full day's work for a full day's wage. No slacking or taking the easy way. Show up on time. Stay until the end of the day. Finish what you start. Be respectful of your coworkers. Show respect to your boss even though you may disagree with him. He is your boss. If you feel the need to disagree, do it with respect. And most importantly, remember to bring more value than you cost.

> Give everything you do everything
> you've got. Growing a pair is not about
> giving half-assed effort.

Grow a pair with your boss.

Does your boss belittle you? Does he criticize you, not your work? Why? I'm betting it's because you allow it. Stop. He or she may be your boss and deserve your respect simply for that reason, but that does not mean that you need to allow him or her to mistreat you on a personal level. Learn to stand up for yourself. Document the occurrences in detail, schedule a time to talk with your boss, and make your grievances known in a polite, courteous, respectful way. Take all emotion out of the equation. Be serious and stand your ground about what you consider fair and unfair. Have a discussion about what is happening and what you would like to see happen in the future. If it doesn't work, take the documentation to your HR department. If you work in a small company that doesn't have an HR department, then consider working someplace else where you can retain your dignity. If the situation is serious enough, consult an attorney.

Grow a pair with your coworkers.

When your coworker is slacking off and you have to work extra hard to make up the difference, speak up! Don't be a tattletale and go whining to your boss—at least not at first. Have enough of a pair to go directly to the person you have an issue with and point out the problem. Be nice but firm, don't whine, know what you are talking about, and explain your issue to them. Explain what you want to see happen and explain the consequences if things don't change. Then if it doesn't happen, deliver on the consequences. That's the appropriate time to approach your supervisor.

Grow a pair as a leader/manager.

True leaders don't lead by committee or focus group. They don't lead by consensus or by popularity polls. A real leader confidently makes the decision he or she feels is best for the overall success of the organization. He doesn't worry about whether his decision will be liked or approved of by all. He makes his decision based on the facts and by following his gut. He takes full responsibility for his decision and shares the glory and absorbs the blame when it doesn't go well. A true leader has a pair. A true leader will communicate what she expects, teach her followers how to deliver what she expects, and then impose consequences when she doesn't get what she expects. You never have to wonder how a true leader feels or where he stands on an issue, as his position will be very clear.

Grow a pair with your employees.

The first and most fundamental responsibility you have to your employer and to your customers is to deal effectively with your employees. To do that, set high expectations, communicate them, and impose consequences for poor performance. People will either live up to or down to the expectations you have of them. If people are not living up to the expectations you have of them, perhaps it is because you haven't clearly communicated what you expect. You should have a job description written down for every position at your company. This job description clearly states the requirements associated with the job. It is specific, it is task oriented, it is measurable, and the focus is on the results that you expect from anyone working in that position. This description should be read to and discussed with the employee when they are hired or promoted to ensure that it is completely understood and agreed upon. This will eliminate any confusion about what is expected and your employee will never be able to use the excuse "I didn't know."

At the same time that you are communicating what you expect, you must also communicate clearly what happens when you don't get what you expect and what happens when you do get what you expect. These are called consequences. All actions have a consequence and this must be communicated clearly in advance in order to improve performance and reduce disappointment. In other words, as you explain the job description, you must explain what happens to your employee if they do not deliver on each of the items in the job description. They need to understand that their work affects others in the company and that sub-par work can put the entire company in a bad position and might cost the company its standing with the customer. Even the janitor has an impact on the customer and they need to understand that and know what happens when they don't do their job according to what has been communicated to them. Every employee in your company needs to understand consequences: "If this happens, then this happens." Or, "If this doesn't happen, then this has to happen." As a manager you owe each employee this level of communication. It establishes a benchmark for acceptable performance and a standard for managing in the future.

Once you have communicated your expectations with your employees and communicated the consequences of what happens when they deliver or don't deliver, you have to make sure that they have the skills they need to do the job. Telling an employee that you expect them to do a job and that there will be consequences for poor performance, without taking the time to make sure they actually can do what you expect, is unforgivable. Take the time to do the training. Once you are sure they understand what is expected and you are confident that they have the skills to do the job, they can be held accountable for their results.

Now that you have taught your employees how to deliver on the expectations you have set for them, you have to be prepared to deliver the consequences when you don't get what you expect. Sadly, because we have become so fearful of being sued, few leaders and managers are willing to deliver the consequences that come with poor performance. Bad employees with poor work habits and no work ethic run most businesses today. Many workers come to work late, put in just enough work to get by, and have little respect for their coworkers or management and even less respect for their customers. They figure that management and the HR department wouldn't risk a lawsuit and they think they can get by with damn near any type of poor behavior without any consequences. Even if they are reprimanded, those who are protected by a union know that the union will fight for them regardless of how abhorrent their behavior has been.

Leaders, managers, HR departments, pay attention here: Grow a pair! Fire every employee who gives you less than you pay them for. Stop tolerating poor performance in every single employee down to the smallest violation. No more coming in late, no more long lunch hours, and no more half-assed effort in exchange for full pay. Take your business back from the lousy, disinterested employees and put it in the hands of those who care about serving the customer, deliver excellence in all they do, and understand the concept of adding value to your company through hard work. Will you get sued? Maybe. Cover your bases by documenting all bad behavior well. Don't be stupid about this stuff as we all have guidelines that must be followed. But never let anything or anyone stand in your way when it comes to dealing with a lousy employee. Fire them and fight them on the outside of your business rather than letting them destroy your business from the inside.

Grow a pair with your customers.

Customers are the lifeblood of your company. I use the word "customer" but the same applies whether you call them the client, the patient, or in my case, the audience or reader—they are customers. I always prefer to use the word "customer" because it boils things down to a basic relationship: We all understand that customers spend money to keep the business in business. The image of a money exchange taking place is something that people with "clients" and "patients" need to understand a bit better. The point is, it's their money that keeps you in business. However, some customers are frankly a pain in the ass. That can be tolerated up to a point. But there is a line that you cannot allow a customer to cross. Disrespecting your employees is one of those lines. No customer should be allowed to cuss at your employees or speak abusively to them. Don't tolerate it. Be polite but explain that that is not acceptable behavior. When you let a customer push you around, they take advantage of you. They don't respect you. They use you. The old saying that "the customer is always right" is true, but sometimes that customer is not right for you.

Customers who continually pay you late or beat you

up on price are not customers that are worth having. Don't tolerate it. Explain to them that you will not be able to do business with them if they continue to disrespect your business by paying you late or by showing a lack of respect for your pricing. Any customer can have a financial issue from time to time and that is understandable. However, you can afford to do without the customer that turns into an abuser. And if you decide that you honestly can't afford to do without that abusive customer, don't complain, because you have taught them that it's perfectly fine to treat you in that manner.

Grow a pair with the people you spend your money with.

To pay for bad service is stupid. Don't do it. Complain.

If you let bad service slide without commenting in an appropriate way, then you are being unfair to the next customer. Don't you wish the guy who experienced the same bad service you did had complained until he got it fixed, as it might have saved you the pain?

Example: I walked into a restaurant with some friends and was seated at a table. The waiter approached the table and said, "Don't expect very good service tonight. I'm having a really bad day. Now what can I get you?" I replied, "You can get me a new waiter." He looked at me like I was an idiot and said, "I can't do that. This is my table." I said, "You see, that's where you are confused. This is *my* table. I'm paying for the food and the service. That makes it mine, not yours, so get me another waiter." He wandered off and the manager came over and asked what the problem was. I said that there wasn't a problem but I wanted a new waiter. I told him what the waiter had said to us and then explained how stupid it would be for me to pay for bad service that I had been promised in advance. The manager looked at me in sort of a bewildered way and said, "But he really is having a bad day."

Yep, that actually happened—people in the service business expecting me to accept bad service because they are having a bad day. Get something straight: No one cares about the day you are having. You aren't paid to have a good day or a bad day. You are paid to do your job and serve your customers. How you feel about it has nothing to do with it. And it certainly isn't relevant to your customer.

Most people wouldn't have said a word about any of this. They would have accepted the bad service and then left a 15 or 20 percent tip just because they don't have a pair and are weenies. They are concerned that the waiter, who served them poorly, might think less of them if they don't tip well. Look what a mess we have become!

Another example: A guy came walking into my backyard one morning. My dogs were inside the house, looking out at him and barking like crazy, watching him walk around their yard. I walked out and said, "Can I help you?" He said that he was with the gas company and needed to check my gas meter for leaks and wanted to know where the meter was. I asked him why he didn't just ring my doorbell and ask me where the meter was. I told him that walking into a man's backyard unannounced was an excellent way to either get bitten by a dog or shot. He said, "Well, I'm wearing this green vest." I asked him how much good the vest would do him in either of those scenarios. I then told him to go away and come back when he could approach my house professionally. I can guarantee you that most folks would have listened to his explanation and not said anything negative to him. That's ridiculous. First, it takes more than a green vest to prove he is who he says he is. Besides, that green vest isn't bulletproof, is it? Or dog-bite proof either! Second, it's unacceptable to allow someone to walk into your yard unannounced or unidentified. Most of all, it is unprofessional for the company that sent him out to allow this to happen. Yet most people would avoid confrontation in this situation even if their safety were at stake.

Speak up directly to the person delivering the bad service. If you aren't satisfied with the response, speak to a manager. If you still aren't satisfied, take it up the ladder until you are. Remember when complaining that everyone has a boss. If you don't receive satisfaction in rectifying a situation, keep going up the chain of command until you do.

You can also blog about your experience. You can use services like Yelp to critique the business. Tweet about it. Facebook about it. Social media has a purpose beyond posting pictures of your vacation or cute videos of kitty cats!

THE KEY TO BUSINESS SUCCESS: KEEP MOVING.

"A rolling stone gathers no moss." Heard that one before? If not, where have you been? It means that you need to keep moving. It means that if you sit in one place too long, grubby little things will overtake you and cause you to get stuck. So move! Never stay in one place for too long because you will get stuck there.

Even if the place you are in is a very good place, you are going to want to stay on the move. Success can be your biggest enemy if you wallow too long in it. I know because I've done this. I have been extremely successful. I had been the hardest working man in the speaking industry for years. I created more products, gave more speeches, and got on more planes than probably any five busy speakers put together. I was about the busiest marketer in the personal development industry, with people on the phone calling meeting planners and speakers bureaus to keep me on stages around the world. I had a person who did nothing but handle my travel arrangements and ship my books to my engagements. All of this work came to a peak with me starring in my own television show and writing five bestsellers, all while doing close to a hundred speeches a year.

And then the market changed. A recession happened. My whole industry went into a huge slump. People stopped having big meetings and the ones who were having meetings stopped spending big bucks on speakers. The publishing industry and book business took a nosedive. Publishers were laying off employees, and major bookstores were going out of business. Tablets and e-books began their takeover and the traditional paper-and-ink book started down the path of the dinosaur. Where did that leave a guy who makes his living doing speeches at huge meetings and writing bestselling books? With an empty calendar and not much going on.

Because of my huge success coming off of a popular television show, three national commercials, regular appearances on television news shows and three television specials, plus five bestsellers in a row, I hadn't had to market myself for a good long while. My calendar was packed out two years in advance, so why bother marketing, right? I was so used to being popular and successful that I didn't even notice when my own slump was starting. And then it happened. It all ran out. The bookings were completed and I found myself with an empty calendar. My success had become my enemy. I had become complacent, resting on my laurels, relying on my momentum, and then I found myself basically unemployed.

So I did what every person should do when they find themselves in a tough spot: I circled the wagons and went back to work. I regrouped and reinvented the way I did business. I got good at marketing via the Internet, something I hadn't kept up with at all. I used social media to expand my business and my brand. I overhauled my website. I started offering other speaking services as part of my product line. Instead of just a keynote, I started offering breakout sessions as add-ons. I created video training programs. I started writing and selling articles. I capitalized on my "strategic alliances," which is fancy talk for saying I called my buddies and started exploring ways that we could utilize each other's skills to expand our market share, which is more fancy talk for figuring out ways to make some money working together. As a result I created programs like A Year of Success and A Year of Business Success. These are year-long programs I produced with some colleagues who are also success/business experts, which deliver one video each week along with an action plan to help you achieve more success either personally or professionally. To sum it up, I got smarter, leaner, and yes, even meaner. In other words, I grew a pair and faced the situation head on and got moving again.

I was fortunate. I had done a lot of smart stuff during my most successful years. I had stashed some cash, invested well, and saved. Many people found themselves in a slump when the recession hit and didn't do any of those things. These folks were in trouble. You have probably heard lots of stories about people who were caught in a bad spot when the recession hit. You might be one of those stories. I know lots of really successful people who have very similar stories to mine who did just what I did: They got moving again. And it renewed their spirit and invigorated them and allowed them to begin again with new energy.

The lesson from all of this is to stay moving. If you are in a slump, action changes things. If you are in a really successful place right now, stay aware, stay current, and keep your eyes on the next thing you are going to do to maintain your success.

The best way to get ahead is to move your behind.

Principles for Growing a Pair in Business

List time again. Write down your top five business principles that you refuse to compromise:

1. _____

    _____

2. _____

    _____

3. _____

_____

4. _____

_____

5. _____

_____

GROW A PAIR AT HOME

Growing a pair isn't just about you, your money, and your business; it's also about your home and the people in it. Homes need to be run—they don't run by themselves. Homes need leaders who have a pair and will stand up for what is right and acceptable within the boundaries of the home. You have to have a pair in what you stand for as a leader in your family, with your spouse, with your kids, and with your friends. Let's look at each of those areas.

GROW A PAIR WITH YOUR SPOUSE.

Many guys should just go ahead and change their name to Mat, as in DoorMat, since they let their women walk all over them. You allow yourself to be talked to like you are a dog. No woman likes that. She may get off on the power trip of treating you like crap but she doesn't respect you, and any relationship that isn't built on mutual respect is worthless.

The same goes for women. Women, I tire of the

stupid Facebook/Twitter comments about how your man treats you badly. You *let* him! Do you not see that? Holy crap, people—step up! Grow a pair and decide how you will be treated and then hold people to that standard. It's your choice!

Another thing: Women, when you get ready to go out to dinner and he says, "I'm ready," and you are in your little black dress and he has on a T-shirt and shorts and flip-flops, grow a pair and say, "No, you're not ready!" Guys, when she says, "Does this dress make me look fat?" tell her the truth. But won't that hurt her feelings? Not as much as going out in a dress that makes her look fat!

If you hate one of the things your spouse loves, it's okay to say so. My wife loves some movies that I would rather gouge my eyes out with a carrot stick than see, and she respects that and goes alone. I grew a pair and admitted to her that I hated those movies she loves and she grew a pair and said it didn't matter because she would just go alone. We both won. My wife has some friends I can't stand. I told her. Now I don't have to be around them. I have this great shirt but my wife finally said, "Enough, I hate that shirt and you need to get rid of it." I said fine, you will never see it again and now I wear it only when I travel. These all may seem like silly, trivial little things and they are, but I see couples every day that pretend to love what the other person does even though they hate it. We don't bother to pretend. Of course, it's also okay to suck it up and do something you hate sometimes just because your spouse loves it. That's just being a good partner.

When your spouse wants to spend money and you know that your family can't afford to do it and should be saving your money or paying bills, grow a pair and say no. One of the biggest problems we have in this country is overspending and it's because people can't say no to themselves or to their spouse. Every couple that has a spender has an enabler.

GROW A PAIR AS A PARENT.

Too many parents don't understand what it means to be a parent. I wrote a whole book on this subject entitled *Your Kids Are Your Own Fault*. In this book, I talk about how bad parenting is to blame for almost all of the world's problems. From bad service to the housing crisis to entitlement issues, bad parenting is to blame. Therefore, if you want to take back our world and reverse the collision course with disaster that our society is on, grow a pair and be a real parent.

How do you become a real parent with a pair? If you want the full story on how to be a better parent, read my full book on the subject, but in the meantime here is the short course:

Spend time with your kids.
As much as you can. As the father of two grown boys, I look back wishing I had spent more time with them

when they were little boys simply because they don't stay little boys for long. I wish I had said no to working so much and putting things first that at the time seemed just so important to me but that now I know weren't that important at all. How do I know they weren't important? I don't remember them. I remember almost all of the fun I had with my kids, camping and wrestling in the yard and going on long walks talking about life and dogs and girls and cowboys, but I don't remember a thing about the work that seemed more important than doing that stuff. It takes a pair to say no to the distractions and to put your kids ahead of those distractions.

Talk to your kids.

That means talk about more than just the fun stuff. You have to talk about the tough stuff. Talk to them about sex. That's a tough conversation. But considering the teen pregnancy rates and the STD rates, it's a conversation that should be had early and often. It is your responsibility to teach your kids what they need to know and you can't trust the school system to do your work. And you certainly don't want their sexual education to come from their friends, do you? Have the sex talk.

Talk to your kids about money. That probably means that you ought to talk to yourself about money first. Make sure that you know what a budget is and are using one so you can teach your kids the importance of living on less than they earn. Teach them about saving, investing, and enjoying their money. Teach them that having money is even more fun than spending money. Talk to your kid often. It's staggering how little parents actually talk to their children. And when you are talking to them, tell them that you love them. Even when you are secretly wanting to strangle them for the stupid stuff they are doing, tell them you love them. Love is unconditional. Your approval is up for grabs based on their behavior. You can disapprove of their behavior and still communicate that you love them in spite of it.

Be tough on your kids.

Not mean, not ridiculous, and not a nag. But tough enough to let them know exactly what you expect from them. And expect a lot from them. Constantly let them know that they can do more than they think they can do. Encourage them to stretch and grow, and teach them that growth is painful but rewarding. It's easy to let your kids run wild and raise themselves, hoping that the school or the teacher or even the parent down the street will do the job. It's easier to leave your parenting to MTV or VH1 or *Entertainment Tonight*. But then you end up with kids who look and talk and act like Snooki—is that what you want? Be tough enough to tell your kids no and to impose consequences. Be tough enough not to give in and weaken when they beg and plead to go to the party even when they are grounded. Grow a pair and show that you are not their BFF but their parent.

When it comes to teenagers, have a *big* pair.

Teenagers want you the least when they need you the most. Don't let them slip away just because they are so difficult to get along with. Teenagers are a total pain in the butt; it's their job. It's your job to be tough on them, expect a lot from them, impose the tough consequences when they mess up, and love them through it all. Oh yeah, and close the door to their bedroom. It's a mess and you aren't going to fix that. Pick a bigger battle!

Take control of your family and be the parent that your kids will respect. They won't always love you for it and they will sometimes even scream that they hate you for it, but they will learn to respect you for it. Remember, you aren't raising kids, you are training adults. Be strong enough to teach your kids what it takes to be a successful adult. That's a big assignment. That's an assignment that requires a pair!

TEACH YOUR KIDS TO GROW A PAIR.

Parents are to blame for the fact that our new (not improved) entitled generation doesn't have a pair. Parents are overprotective, overindulgent, and have very low expectations. Yes, there are exceptions and I hope you are one. But the exceptions are few. You will know that's true by looking around at the number of people who believe the world owes them a living, owes them health care, a fat salary, a house, a car, and 265 channels of sniveling idiots who are famous for being famous.

I carry my pair in a wheelbarrow. My mama and daddy taught me how to do that. They taught me that self-respect comes from standing up for myself. They taught me to speak up, stand up, and never allow myself to be abused verbally, mentally, or physically. They taught me how to work, earn, spend, and save. They taught me that truth and integrity and honesty were the most important things. Everything I am today is because of the foundation that was built from the teachings of my parents. Everything. I am so thankful they had a pair and were the parents that I needed them to be.

Make your kids do the right thing and teach them what the right thing is. Examine that statement. I said *make* your kids do the right thing. Yes, make. They are kids. You are the parent. You are in control. Wait, you're not in control? Then you are a lousy parent.

It is your responsibility as a parent to teach your kids what they need to know: manners, a strong work ethic, how to get along with people, how to stand up for themselves; honesty and integrity; how to handle money, sex, and relationships; how the world works . . . you know, the basics. What's the best way to do this? Read my book, *Your Kids Are Your Own Fault*, but first, follow these basic steps:

First, live it.

Kids will learn more by watching you and the example you set than from any other thing. You can't live by the old, incredibly stupid saying, "Do as I say, not as I do." Kids are smarter than that and won't respect you if that is your parenting philosophy. Be the person you want your kids to grow up and become.

Second, talk to them about it.

Communicate what you expect from your kids. Talk to them about the behavior you want, model that behavior for them, and grab every teachable moment you can to have a discussion about how they can use these lessons in every area of their lives.

Third, recognize and honor those things in other people.

When you see a great example from someone else, take that moment to have a quick talk. Talk about how you admire their behavior and why. Talk about what you learned from their story and example. Your kids will look for role models. Help them find good ones by admiring others for living an exemplary life.

Fourth, set high expectations.

Challenge your children with high expectations. Not unreasonable expectations, but the kind that make them push a bit to achieve. Growth, while painful, is always a good thing, so set goals with your kids that will allow them to grow and then show them how to achieve those goals.

Fifth, impose consequences when they don't live up to those expectations.

Every action has a consequence. Winning is a consequence. So is losing. They are both a part of life. You wouldn't cheat your kids of the glory of winning, would you? Of course not. Don't cheat your kids of the pain that comes from losing either.

Get your kids involved in sports.

I recently did a television interview about how yoga is the fastest growing sport in America for children. I made it clear that I don't believe that yoga is a sport. Yoga is many things and I'm all for it and think it is a great exercise program, but please let's not confuse parents or children by allowing them to think that yoga is a sport. Let me make it easy for you: If no one is keeping score, it's not a sport.

In sports, there is a winner and a loser. In many sports, you are part of a team. You have to learn to get along with others and work together. Teamwork teaches you how to work together for a common goal. In sports, you get knocked down and you have to learn how to get back up. Great life lessons for sure. You also learn that there are people who are better than you, bigger than you, and more practiced and prepared than you. Again, a lot like life. Sports will teach your kids valuable life lessons. Solitary exercise like yoga, while valuable with lessons of its own, won't teach those lessons. But some parents are attracted to yoga and similar solitary exercise programs because they are overly protective of their precious little ones. They don't want to see their kids knocked down or hurt and they certainly don't want them to ever experience the pain of losing. That's a mistake. Involve your kids in competitive sports so they learn life lessons that will help them as they grow up and will prepare them for the real world.

So be a real parent, and grow a pair. Stop being your kids' friend. Be their parent and do your job. Your family is not a democracy; it's an absolute monarchy and you are in charge. Take charge like a leader is supposed to do.

Teach them how to deal with bullies.

It's a popular topic these days. Books, talk shows, and even a movie talk about the effects of bullying. We are passing laws to make bullying illegal. Stupidly, people believe you can legislate against bullying behavior. You can't. There will always be bullies. There always have been and there always will be. You can't outlaw bullying. You can't teach other kids not to bully your kid, but you can teach your kid not to be a victim. Remember this when it comes to bullying: You can't have a bully without a victim.

Most folks would think that bullies and loud-mouths and other rude jerks have a pair. Don't kid

yourself. The truth is just the opposite. The loud-mouthed jackasses pushing others around don't have a pair; they are actually compensating for not having a pair with their rude behavior. Much like the loud-mouth with the bright red sports car is compensating for his shortcomings. Bullies are cowards. Grow a pair and stand up to them. Teach your kids to stand up to the bully and stop being a victim. Teach them this lesson when they are young; otherwise, they will spend the rest of their lives being a victim. Bullies exist at every stage of life: in school, on the playground, in families, on the ball field, at work, in the office—you name it and there will be a bully.

When I was a little scrawny kid who was being picked on by a bully, my dad told me, "It's better to nurse a bloody nose than lose your dignity." That was a valuable lesson. I have used this lesson in life and business many times. Sometimes I had to nurse a bloody nose but I always kept my dignity.

Teach them how *not* to deal with cyberbullies.

Let me begin by saying that as a parent, it is your job to monitor your kid's online activity. It takes time and you have to be persistent and it's easier not to do it, which is the route most parents take. Don't be that parent. It is imperative that you do your job and monitor what your kid is doing online. There are bad people out there ready to prey on unsuspecting kids and you need to be sure that doesn't happen to your kids. Be their friend on Facebook whether they want you to or not. Check their search history and their e-mails until they are old enough for it to become invasive and until they have proven that they are trustworthy. That means you have to teach them how to use the Internet for good things like learning and for communication.

On to the issue of cyberbullying—seriously? In my opinion, this one is ridiculous. You allow your kids to care about what others say about them online? And don't say, "Yeah, Larry, but it's a different world out there now." I get it. I make a good part of my living online. I get attacked every day by idiots online that say horrible things to me and about me. I don't much care. When I do care a little, I tell them they are idiots and move on. If they truly annoy me, I block them. That doesn't stop them from saying bad things about me, but it stops me from being aware of it. My parents taught me when I was young not to care what other people said. That is why I have this attitude today. When you look at the person saying the bad stuff as an idiot, then their opinion doesn't matter. When you give credence to their stupidity, it can eat you up. Don't give stupid remarks made by stupid people any credence. People have always said stupid things. There have always been "verbal bullies": people who use words to hurt others. This is no different. This is just the new tool used by tools to say hurtful things. Teach your kids to rise above it. Yeah, I know it's not easy. Yeah, I know that they are really hurt and feel humiliated. Big deal. Get over it.

Never argue with stupid people. They will drag you down
to their level and then beat you with experience.
—Mark Twain

"Stick and stones may break my bones but words
will never hurt me." Remember that? It was a little
song we sang when I was a kid. I believed it. Still do.
They are *words*! Words being spoken by stupid people
who are seeking to build themselves up by tearing you
down. Don't allow your kid to fall victim to words.
Teach your kid that it is the other kid who has the
problem, not him. Teach your kid that there are stupid,
hurtful people in the world. There always have been
and there always will be. This lesson must be learned as
a child. It is your responsibility as a parent to teach it. I
am sure you see grown men and women who live and
die based on the way they are seen by others. These are
pitiful, sad people with no self-respect. They have
placed their happiness in the hands of someone else,
which is a total waste of time.

Kick your grown kids out!

The singular goal of parenting should be to raise an
independent adult that can function in the world all on
their own. In other words, you raise your kids so they
will grow up and *leave*! If your thirty-year-old kid is
still living with you, you failed as a parent. The recent
phenomenon of grown children still living at home is
proof that parents don't have a pair. A recent study by

the National Endowment for Financial Education and Forbes.com says that nearly 60 percent of parents provide financial support to their adult children who are no longer in school. There may be a few cases where this might be necessary for a very limited period of time, but my gut tells me that about 99 percent of the time, it is the result of parents who don't have enough of a pair to tell their lazy kids to get out and make a living. The same study says that nearly half of the parents provide the financial support because they struggled and don't want their kids to have to struggle. Did they forget that it's learning how to survive the struggles that made them successful in the first place? Do they not see that robbing their kids of the same struggles is crippling them and doing them a huge disservice? Do they not realize that they are sacrificing the life they worked so hard for so many years to create for themselves in order to take care of a kid who isn't willing to take care of himself? Guess not. Don't be one of these enabling parents. When your kids are out of school, they are on their own. If you do your job as a parent from the time your kids are babies, they will have the skills to survive and even thrive regardless of the challenges they face in the world. If they can't, you didn't do your job as a parent, but you can't make up for that by continuing to support them. Grow a pair and allow them to do the same.

GROW A PAIR WITH YOUR FRIENDS.

Do your friends hurt your feelings? Do they constantly say things to you like, "I'm going to tell you this for your own good . . ."? Trust me, they aren't telling you anything for your own good; they are telling you for *their* own good. A real friend won't make excuses and soft-shoe the truth. A friend will say something more along the lines of, "You're being an idiot. Stop it. You are better than this; you know better and I expect more from you."

True friends show respect for each other. They show up when they say they will and they honor their commitments to one another. I have some friends who just can't seem to be on time. My wife and I love to cook and we invite them for dinner at seven P.M. We have planned, have things cooking, and have timed everything just right. The appetizers are ready to go at seven and dinner is usually set for eight P.M. The food is in the oven or on my smoker, and timing is everything when you are serious about your food. Then they show up at seven thirty with some lame-ass excuse. I'll buy your excuse once, but every time is unacceptable. At seven thirty, the appetizers are cold and the food has to be delayed and will probably end up being overcooked. I'm ticked. I buy good products, I do a good job cooking, and I take having people over very seriously, out of respect. To show up late is disrespectful. When I pointed this out after a couple of times, I got the old "we are just fashionably late." What a load of crap. There is nothing fashionable about being late. Late is rude. Late is disrespectful. I then made it clear that in the future, if they were unwilling to respect the work that my wife and I went through to cook a great meal by showing up on time, they would never be invited again. The next time I invited them over they were late again. They have never been invited again and never will be. The interesting thing to me is that when I tell that story, some people consider me the rude one, saying that I should make allowances for their lateness, as that is just the kind of people they are. That's correct. That is the kind of person they are: late, rude, and disrespectful. I choose not to allow that in my life. So grow a pair and make a decision about the kind of friends you want involved in your life.

Some friends are like belts: You eventually outgrow them.

Principles for Growing a Pair at Home

Just as you should never compromise your principles as an individual, with your money, or in your business, you must never compromise your principles within your home.

Write down your top three principles
regarding your relationship with your spouse:

1. _____

_____

2. _____

_____

3. _____

_____

Write down your top three principles
regarding your relationship with your kids:

1. _____

_____

2. _____

_____

3. _____

_____

Write down your top three principles
regarding your relationship with your friends:

1. _____

_____

2. _____

_____

3. _____

_____

BE A CITIZEN WITH
A PAIR

So far, I've talked about growing a pair as an individual, with your family, in your business, and with your money. Now, let's broaden our scope and talk about the changes you can make in your own behavior that will have a positive effect on society.

CONFRONT WRONG.

Don't let people mistreat others. Don't ignore bad behavior. Don't say, "It's none of my business." It *is* your business when you find someone stealing, lying, or mistreating another person. Speak up. Take action. Intervene.

I was on a plane recently when they announced that there would be a slight delay due to a mechanical problem. Yes, this is an inconvenience to everyone, and no one was happy about the situation. Connections might be missed and the moans were audible from all over the plane. While I hate delays as much as the next guy, I'm also not eager to fly on a plane with mechanical problems. But the guy in front of me became furious. He started screaming at the flight attendant. He was telling her how stupid she was and what a stupid airline she worked for and on and on. She was doing her best to be polite but this jerk wouldn't let up. I shook his chair really hard to get his attention and when he turned his head toward me, I told him to shut up and to stop yelling at her as it clearly wasn't her fault and that he was making an ass of himself. He said, "Who the hell do you think you are?" I told him I was the guy telling him to stop making an ass of himself and to behave. At that point, the guy across the aisle from him said, "Yeah!" and a couple more grumbles of support came from the seats around me too. A look came across his face and he said, "I'm sorry." I said, "Tell her, not me." And he did. And she thanked me. It took thirty seconds and a pair to stop someone from being screamed at and belittled. And it reminded that guy that he needed to check himself. This is one of the many times that I have confronted wrong with my pair.

SPEAK UP FOR THOSE WHO CAN'T.

Some people can't speak up for themselves. The elderly, little kids, and even animals often need people with a pair to stand up and speak up on their behalf. For instance: A woman in Phoenix in a pizza restaurant with her kids was seen by another diner pouring beer from her pitcher into her two-year-old's sippy cup. The baby drank the beer and soon after fell out of his chair. Thankfully, the diner did the right thing and called the police and the mother was arrested and charged with child abuse. At the time of this writing, the case is still pending.

Sadly, most people see something like this and while appalled, wouldn't want to become involved or cause a scene or go through the hassle of making the call to the authorities. But people with a pair will put justice ahead of their own convenience and do the right thing.

My belief is that if you witness abuse, bullying, or other mistreatment of another person or animal and don't step up to stop it, you are just as guilty as the one doing the mistreating. Yes, you are guilty because your lack of action allowed the behavior to continue. Your lack of a pair, your cowardice, your need to put your convenience ahead of the well-being of others makes you guilty. Remember this the next time you see abuse of another person or animal: If you don't step up, it's on you!

DON'T BE A SHEEPLE.

That's right: sheeple. Is that term new to you? Sheeple are people who voluntarily acquiesce to the beliefs or opinions of another person or a political party or religious belief without any critical analysis or research or thought process of their own. To simplify, it's people who act like sheep. They follow the leader—pretty much any leader—simply because it takes too much effort to form opinions of their own. Sheeple don't have a pair. Instead, they count on their guru to have the pair and to guide them in the right direction. That can be very dangerous, especially when the guru in the lead turns out to be a bad guy.

James Ray, the motivational guru, had plenty of sheeple. His sheeple were willing to set their own safety aside and to follow him into a sweat lodge. And some of them ended up dead as a result of it. Jim Jones had sheeple follow him in Jonestown who were willing to drink poisoned Kool-Aid, and all ended up dead. In fact, "drinking the Kool-Aid" has become part of our vernacular, meaning to follow a person or their philosophy without any critical examination. Most popular politicians and religious figures have sheeple. Some would argue that even I have sheeple. Lord, I hope not. I don't want them. I want independent thinkers who are able to listen to what I have to say, then agree or disagree on the merits of my words and my argument. Don't be a sheeple for anyone or any group or movement. Learn to think for yourself.

GROW A PAIR WITH YOUR GOVERNMENT.

We love to complain about the government. It seems to occupy most of our discussions these days. People either hate the government or love the government. If you rely on the government for your living, then you probably like the government a lot. If you feel like the government is taking more than their share of your income and spending it unwisely, you probably aren't so wild about the government. That basic disagreement is the cause of most of the rhetoric we hear on cable television news programs. Talk, talk, talk. I am betting that you get as tired of it as I do. And most of the talk isn't intelligent conversation between informed people; instead, it's griping. The fact is, pretty much all people do about the government is gripe about it. They don't take the actions needed to fix their government.

How do you fix your government? The first thing you could do, if you are a glutton for punishment, is to run for office yourself. If you are willing to do that, then you really do have a pair and I applaud you for even having the thought. That is how things really change: honest, hardworking people who are willing to go get involved on a first-hand basis and run for office. However, if you aren't willing to do that, the least you can do is vote.

Before you vote, educate yourself. I'm always amazed when people clearly don't know the issues and don't know the candidates. I am at the point where I believe there should be an intelligence test given to all prospective voters just to make sure they are qualified to have a vote. Some of us consider our voting a privilege and don't take any part of it for granted. We study the issues.

We study the candidates. We do more than toe the party line and instead vote our conscience regardless of party affiliation in hopes of finding politicians who are just a little better than the last crop and who will move us back toward a place of integrity and common sense.

Bare minimum, vote for politicians who have a pair and who will say no to spending money we don't have. Vote for politicians who are more interested in fixing things than getting elected. Vote for judges who are tough on crime and tougher on criminals. In other words, vote for people who stand up for their beliefs and yours.

Every time I write about voting, people tell me that voting doesn't matter. Folks, if you believe that, you are a complete idiot. Voting is the only thing that matters when it comes to changing the government. You can't overthrow a bad government in this day and age in the United States of America. You can only vote out one set of bozos in the hopes of getting a better set. People tell me that we are just trading one set of crooks for another. Okay, not a big argument from me on this one. That may truly be the case. But the key is to keep voting out the bad guys for a set of less bad guys until hopefully we end up somewhere down the road with some okay guys.

Will we ever get exactly what we need? No. Will we ever get what we all want? Definitely not. But whether you like it or not, or want to believe it or not, we always get exactly what we deserve because we get what we vote for or don't vote for.

Can I guarantee that things will change if you vote? No. But I can guarantee that things will never change if you don't vote!

Principles for Being a Citizen with a Pair

This is your last list. It's time for you to think about the principles you will follow to be a better citizen to make your community, your state, your country, and the world a better place to live for all of us.

1. _____

   _____

2. _____

   _____

3. _____

   _____

4. _____

   _____

5. _____

   _____

"I CAN'T DO THIS."

At this point there are going to be many of you saying, "But, Larry, I just can't do this. All of this is against my nature!"

I don't know your "nature" so I am not going to argue with you about that. But to tell you the truth, I believe "against my nature" is just a cop-out. If you are saying to yourself that you can't grow a pair and do the things I have laid out here so far, I want you to know that you can do whatever you want to do if your will is strong enough. Let me repeat myself: If you want to grow a pair badly enough you can do it. The desperate need for this kind of improvement in our society should be reason enough <u>for you</u> to make the change. Our government, our businesses, and our families are a mess because we have convinced ourselves that it is rude and mean to be strong and assertive. As a result, we have become weak, and all of society suffers.

But if you don't buy that and still want to argue that you just can't do any of this, let me just say this to you and you can wallow around with this thought for a while:

Can't usually means won't.

THE BENEFITS OF
GROWING A PAIR

SUCCESS

All of the great entrepreneurs and businesspeople in society became successful because they had a pair. They lived boldly and took risks. People who never grow a pair and live meekly rarely live up to their fullest potential. They are known as nice people who get along with everyone. While being nice and getting along with everyone is great, it isn't usually enough to create success. Success comes from a willingness to take a bold stand and take action on your thoughts, beliefs, and ideas. And that requires a pair.

BETTER SERVICE

The only way you will ever start to receive good service is when you start to expect it, communicate clearly that you will accept nothing less than good service, and complain appropriately when you don't get it. When

you do those things, you will be amazed at how people start to treat you better.

BETTER KIDS

You want better kids; we all want better kids. When you grow a pair and start standing up against the trend of permissiveness that is taking over our society, you will have better kids. When you start being the kind of parent who firmly teaches and reinforces the building blocks of success in your children, you will know that you are properly preparing them for the real world. You will be teaching them what no school, video game, or television show will ever be able to do.

BETTER FRIENDS

When your friends understand that they don't get to walk all over you or take you for granted, they will stop doing it. When they know what you expect from their friendship, you will find yourself less disappointed in them because they will begin to treat you with the respect you deserve. At the same time, you will become a better friend to people, because growing a pair will make you a person with stronger values who practices what you preach. In addition, you will find that growing a pair causes you to attract better people into your life.

CONFIDENCE

Growing a pair will allow you to carry yourself with more confidence. You will walk taller. You will feel better. You will be healthier. You will be happier. You will find things go your way more often simply because you are more in control of your own life. Confidence can add hair and subtract pounds. It's sexy. Women love confident men and men love confident women. Employers love confident employees. Customers love to be sold to by confident salespeople. Kids appreciate confident parents. People want to do business with confident people. Confidence is a quality that will make you feel great and will benefit those around you.

MONEY

Your chances of having more money increase when you grow a pair. As I have already pointed out, people with a pair tend to be more responsible with their money. They live and work with a higher level of integrity than others, so their results are better. They are also more prone to take risks and become entrepreneurs, which increases their chances of being rich. And when you have a pair, you will be more likely to earn a raise and ask for a raise. If you are a salesperson, you will ask for the sale more often, resulting in more sales and higher commissions.

HAPPINESS

Defined as mental or emotional well-being, happiness is the state of mind that comes from growing a pair. When you are in control of your life, you will feel like you can face anything and work your way through it. Irritating people and unfavorable circumstances are things you know you can deal with. You have the confidence to thrive and survive in the face of anything. You can't be beat. You may get beaten, but you won't be beat! This is the very essence of happiness.

SATISFACTION

Few things are better than just feeling good about yourself and your accomplishments. You get that feeling when you have done something you can be proud of. Growing a pair so you can be in full control of your life will give you that feeling every day in almost everything you do. What could possibly be better?

I was recently at an appointment and had parked in a big garage, the kind where they validate your parking when you are finished. When my meeting was over, the person I was meeting with said, "Do you need validation?" I said, "No, I feel really good about myself." She said, "You do, don't you!" Yes, I do.

PRIDE

There are few things more satisfying than a sense of pride that you did your best. People with a pair do their best. Grow a pair and discover that feeling.

CLARITY

I was once at a dinner party where the host had us play a little game where everyone had to come up with one word that described each of the other people in attendance. The word given to describe my doctor, who was in attendance at the party, was "kind." My wife's word was "loving." Others had words like "funny" and "nice" and even "loud." The worst in my opinion was "sweet." That's not a word that would ever be associated with me! Universally, the group decided that my word was "clarity." Perfect. I agree completely. I credit much of my success to clarity. I know what I believe. It's not an act and I don't put it on like a suit before I go onstage or write a book. What I believe is the very core of who I am. There is no gray area and I am unwavering. Clarity made it easy to be my kid, as my boys never had to wonder how Dad was going to feel about what they had done. They knew. It's the reason the news shows call me to do commentary on a story. They know before they call what I am going to say because I am very clear about my position on things. Clarity—and the courage and confidence that come with it—comes from having a pair.

DIGNITY

Dignity is a state best described as the quality of being worthy, honored, or esteemed. People who have a pair carry themselves with dignity. They expect a high level of treatment and have a feeling of self-worth. They honor themselves by being clear about their beliefs and being willing to stand up for them in any and every situation.

COURAGE

Nothing gives you the courage to tackle the next challenge life throws your way more than being a victor in the last challenge you faced. Growing a pair will make you a victor more often.

RESPECT

The best way to earn the respect of others is to be respectable. What does that mean? Be the person others can count on. Be a person of your word. Be honest, have integrity, stand up for yourself and others, speak well, and speak like you know what you are talking about, and you will prove to others that you are respectable. The results are that you will automatically become more respected.

CHARISMA

People who have a pair are more charismatic. People will want to hang around you because you are decisive and live a life grounded in principles you are willing to take a stand for.

THE SIDE EFFECTS OF
HAVING A PAIR

Do you ever watch those commercials advertising drugs and toward the end the announcer drops his voice a bit and talks really fast as he tells you the many side effects of taking their drug? And at that point you decide that perhaps it's just better to have what you have rather than risk the side effects? That might be the case with growing a pair as well. Growing a pair has side effects and some of those side effects are pretty severe.

Criticism

Believe it or not, people will actually criticize you for taking a stand and having opinions. Get used to it.

The only way to avoid criticism: Say *nothing*. Be *nothing*. Do *nothing*.

You will be called mean, a bully, and a pain in the ass.

It's a damn shame that we have reached a place in our society where speaking truthfully and in a direct way makes people consider you to be mean. I put up with this a lot. I get called mean for telling the truth. The truth isn't mean. The truth isn't kind either. The truth just is. It isn't mean to speak the truth. It may not be comfortable for you to hear the truth, but that's not the fault of the truth and it's not the fault of the person who tells the truth either.

You will be called cocky.

Sadly, people mistake confidence for cockiness. This comes primarily from insecurity. Because they don't feel good about themselves, they are threatened by you feeling good about yourself. Let's be clear: That's their problem, not yours. Weak people are always threatened by confident, strong people who are secure in their own skins. Don't worry about it. (Unless you really are cocky. If that's the case, stop.)

You will be called fearless.

You might think this one is a compliment; it's not. People who have a pair are afraid just like anyone else, but the difference is they don't let fear paralyze them. Instead of running from fear, which is what most people do, they face their fears. They understand that to be fearless is to be an idiot.

We are a fear-based society in pretty much every way. Many religious people live their lives in fear of God's wrath, in constant fear of doing something that will send them to hell. Businesspeople run their businesses based on the fear of going out of business. Fear of being broke is what makes some people rich. People buy insurance out of fear. Parents raise their kids out of fear that they will end up in trouble. Fear of being fat is the reason people exercise. Fear of smelling bad is the reason people bathe. People start to smoke for fear of not fitting in, and they stop smoking for fear of dying. Fear of not fitting in is the reason people buy the latest fashions. Fear of looking old is the reason entire industries exist—it's the reason people get face-lifts, Botox, tummy tucks, and more. Fear of dying is the reason some people never really live. People are afraid of being honest for fear of offending someone. Fear of not being the best paralyzes some people into never acting at all. Fear of not being liked is the major reason most people bother to be nice. Fear of getting fired is the reason most people bother to work while at work. Fear of being late is the reason people wear a watch. Fear is the major motivator for all of the action that takes place in the world. We do almost all we do out of fear of the consequences of not doing it. Fear of a pig farm opening up in the middle of your neighborhood is the reason your town has zoning laws. The list is endless and I could easily go on and on but I won't bother. Bottom line: People say money makes the world go around. They are wrong. Fear makes the world go around.

Solution? There isn't one. In fact, it's not a problem that even needs to be solved. This is just the way the world works. And I am okay with this because I understand that fear is *the* motivator. I always think it is important to understand how things work and to be honest about it and not try to fool yourself. And this is a simple concept that I completely grasp and am totally comfortable with and accepting of.

Besides, we need fear. Imagine the mess we would be in if people feared nothing, if they knew they could get away with things without fear of retribution. Think of the real fear we would all live in if folks weren't afraid that there would be consequences for their bad behavior. Fear is a good thing. Embrace the fear!

That's why I take issue with the motivational bozos telling others to be fearless. I believe we should tell people to be afraid. In fact, be very afraid. Fear works!

Don't kid yourself about why you do what you do; you are afraid of what will happen if you don't do it. Don't kid yourself about why others do what they do. Like you, they are afraid of what will happen if they don't do it. Understanding this simple concept will make you a better salesperson, a better leader/manager, a better parent, and a better spouse and better friend. It will make you a better citizen and a better voter. Understanding that fear is the key motivator to all human behavior will allow you to see the world around you more clearly.

You will be called uncaring.

I get this one a lot too. In my speeches, I stand on stage and tell people I don't care about their problems or if they fix their problems. And I don't. No, really, I don't care. So this one is totally true about me.

If people hear my words and choose to improve their situation, then good for them. I will applaud them and support them. If people hear my words and choose not to do anything, then that is going to be their problem, not mine. My responsibility is to tell the truth, not to make sure people believe it. My responsibility is *to* people, not *for* people.

Some friends and I were talking recently about the state of affairs in our society, and in the middle of one of my "life is your own fault" rants, one of them said to me, "Larry, you don't have any interest in taking care of people, do you?" I told him that he was absolutely correct: I indeed have no interest in taking care of people. I told him that my interest is in teaching people to take care of themselves.

> I have no interest in taking care of people. My interest is in teaching people to take care of themselves.

Having a pair is work.

If you thought that having a pair would make things easier for you, you are wrong. It's more work to have a pair than it is to go through life neutered. It's easier to be stupid and lazy and irresponsible than it is to always do the right thing. Being accountable to yourself and others takes more time, more commitment, more effort, more brain power—in fact, more of just about everything!

Think about it:

It is easier to listen to the political pundits and television news anchors and trust their words completely than it is to study, read, and do the research to discover the truth about a political issue or to actually read one of the bills or proposals you are so vehemently for or against.

It is easier to believe Rush or O'Reilly or Hannity or Olbermann or Maddow or Beck or even Larry Winget than it is to actually do a little fact-checking of your very own. It's work to find the truth out about any issue, so it's easier to just accept what you hear as fact.

It is easier to listen to the preachers and believe every word they say from their pulpit than it is to read the book yourself, or maybe lots of books, and search for your own insight and develop your beliefs based on your own experiences.

It's easier to believe your doctor when he tells you that you should take a pill, rather than doing some research or getting a second opinion to find out if he knows what he is talking about or whether he is padding his pocket and those of the pharmaceutical companies. Standing up to your doctor takes a pair because, well, he's a doctor!

People who do what it takes to grow a pair can't slide by and take the easy way out like regular people get to do. They require a lot from themselves and from others. People with a pair work hard and pay their bills. People with a pair are good parents. People with a pair are concerned about their health and the health of their family. All of these things require a lot of work.

Loss of friends

This is not actually a negative side effect in most cases. If people stop being your friend simply because you have grown a pair, then you haven't lost much! I have lost friends through every growth stage of life. You lose friends when you get a raise. You lose friends when you get a promotion. You lose friends when you decide to get healthy. You lose friends when you start getting smarter or working harder. Every time you improve yourself in any way, you lose friends. And if you lost them because you got better, then they were never your friends to begin with. Write them off and make new friends.

You will have enemies.

A few years ago I was at a big social function where there were many other professional speakers. A fairly successful younger speaker pushed her way into the little group of people I was talking to and said to me, "I'm going to be bigger than you are, Larry Winget." I laughed it off and said, "Well, good for you." I then resumed my conversation with the folks I was talking to. However, she came to make a point and wouldn't let it go. She loudly said, "I'm going to write more books than you, sell more books than you, charge more than you, and be bigger than Larry Winget in every way!" I politely smiled at her and said, "It ain't never going to happen." She was shocked. She looked at me and said, "Why not? Everyone loves me!" I responded, "And that's why it's never going to happen. You can't have rabid fans without rabid enemies. You don't have any enemies and you aren't willing to have any. Your goal is for everyone to love you. Mine is to tell the truth. When you tell the truth, you are going to have people who hate you."

You can't have rabid fans until you are willing to have rabid enemies.

My own willingness to have people hate me is one of the keys to my success. I've had death threats over my stand on personal responsibility. I've had people scream at me while shopping. I regularly get hate mail and get quite a few phone calls as well. I even got a death threat voice mail where the guy saying I should die for the things I say forgot to block his telephone number and it showed up on my caller ID. This guy was proof that alcohol and stupidity don't mix well and a reminder not to drunk-dial. It took me about five minutes on the Internet to figure out who he was, as well as where he lived and worked. You should have heard the call when I phoned him up and introduced myself and asked why I needed to die for encouraging people to take responsibility for their lives, their money, and their kids.

Taking a firm stand will always upset some people. In fact, if no one dislikes you, that's probably a good indication that you aren't taking enough firm stands in your life. And it doesn't really matter what you take a stand over. Jesus took a stand for loving others and they killed him over it. My stand is for personal responsibility. What are you taking a stand for?

> You have enemies? Good. That means you've stood up for
> something, sometime in your life.
> —Usually falsely attributed to Winston Churchill

YOU CAN GROW A PAIR WITHOUT BECOMING A DICK.

Having a pair doesn't mean that you have to behave like a jerk. You don't have to scream, yell, curse, or belittle anyone. You don't need to demean anyone with your words or actions. Growing a pair is about building yourself up, not tearing someone else down. Growing a pair is a state of mind.

Remember, you don't have to go out of your way to prove you have a pair. No bragging is necessary. It's not about pulling them out and showing them off. It's about having this philosophy so ingrained in you that you live uncompromisingly all of the time, in every situation. You don't have to think about when to use your pair and when not to. In fact, you never have to prove that you have a pair or have to think about having a pair. If you really have a pair, people will know without you having to tell them. It will be evident in the way you walk, talk, and act in every way.

Choose your battles. Not everything is a battle. You can have a pair, a big pair, and still not get on a soapbox about every little thing that comes along. Especially when it comes to arguing with stupid people. If there is one thing I have learned over the years, it's that some people really are too stupid to argue with. And as the old saying goes, "When you wrestle a pig, you both get dirty, but the pig likes it."

FINAL THOUGHTS

I have given you plenty of tactics and techniques for growing a pair in your life, at home, with your money, in your business, and in society. I am confident that when you start doing what I've suggested, you will grow a pair and become more successful. In fact, I can guarantee it! *But*—and it's a big ol' but—with success comes failure. Plenty of it. You don't just make up your mind to have a pair and have it suddenly appear. You are going to face many challenges along the way. All success is that way: It comes by experiencing challenges, setbacks, and even total failure. But you don't let failure win. Instead, you rely on your pair to get you off your ass and start again.

Years ago I bought a Harley. I had never owned a motorcycle but I had the look and the attitude and a bike seemed like a great idea. I went into the dealership and paid for it and the guy pulled it around front and said, "There you go!" I told him that I didn't know how to ride it and that someone was going to have to ride it to my house for me. He laughed and said, "You

bought a bike and can't ride it?" I said, "Yep! I did. But don't worry, I'll figure it out."

A little later that day, as I sat in my garage looking at this wonderful machine I had just purchased and trying to figure out how I was going to tell my wife I had bought it, I decided I was ready to take my new toy out for a little spin. I convinced myself that I would be fine . . . after all, how hard could it be? So I hopped on and fired it up. There is nothing quite like a big ol' loud Harley revving up as you set straddle of it!

I slowly pulled out of my driveway and rode down the street. I was thinking, "Okay, this isn't bad; I can do this." Then I turned a corner. I laid the bike on its side and scooted along the pavement. Damn. I had a brand-new Harley and I had ridden only three blocks and I had already wrecked it. I was fine. Not hurt anyplace, except my ego and my pride were badly bruised. I got it back up off the ground and carefully rode it the ten miles back to the Harley dealership. I walked up to their parts-and-service department and told the guy that I had wrecked my bike. He said, "Didn't you just leave here an hour ago?" I told him that I had indeed. He laughed and told me, "Everyone lays their bike down at some point. You are lucky: You got it out of the way early. You'll probably be just fine from now on." He was right. I never had an accident again. I got mine out of the way early.

That's pretty much what it's like when you grow a pair. You are going to lay the thing down and crash at some point. Your ego and your pride will be bruised. But you won't die from growing a pair. You will just get up, dust yourself off, and get back on and do it again until you eventually get it right.

When you begin to live boldly, you increase your likelihood of failure. Some of you are saying, "Then why would you do it?" Because you can't become successful without failure. And you usually can't become amazingly successful without lots of failure!

> It ain't about how hard ya hit. It's about how hard you can get hit and keep moving forward.
> —Sylvester Stallone as Rocky Balboa

ACKNOWLEDGMENTS

Writing the acknowledgments page always makes me feel a lot like the people who receive Academy Awards. They get their Oscar and then in the post–acceptance speech interview backstage they always talk about all the people they forgot to mention. Usually it is their spouse they forget. I am not going to let that happen. I am going to begin by thanking my wife, Rose Mary. I couldn't do what I do without her support. She reads and rereads and works hard to make sure that what I write is readable long before my editor gets the manuscript. But more than that, she puts up with me. Believe me, that's not an easy thing to do. Because I have a pair, a big pair, I speak up often and loudly. For a sweet, quiet peacemaker, that can be embarrassing. But she loves me and believes in me, so she puts up with it. Thank you, Rose Mary.

A few years back, a television producer asked me what brought me to the place I am at, with such a strong set of beliefs of right and wrong and honesty and integrity and the rest of the principles I espouse.

ACKNOWLEDGMENTS

It was an easy answer. I told him I was raised right. And I was. So thanks to Mom and Dad, Dorothy and Henry Winget.

Thanks to my boys, Tyler and Patrick, who remind me that I am not "Larry Winget, that guy on TV," but just a regular guy from Muskogee, Oklahoma, who did good and who is still a dork a good part of the time. They are my barometer for keeping it real.

Thanks to my literary agent, Jay Mandel, with William Morris Endeavor Entertainment, for believing in what I do.

Thanks to my friends at Gotham Books: Bill Shinker, my publisher, along with Lisa Johnson and Beth Parker, who make sure the book gets out there and that people know about it. But most of all, thanks to Jessica Sindler, my editor, who spent a lot of time going back and forth with me, making sure that my words communicated with the reader in the best way possible. I know I can be a frustrating technological dinosaur to work with, and she patiently made it all work.

MORE TOUGH LOVE FROM LARRY

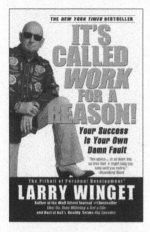

The Pitbull of Personal Development® has more advice on how to take control and get results.

Learn the true meaning of hard work and see the results to prove it.

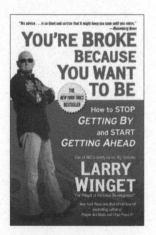

Take control of your finances and find the security you and your family need.

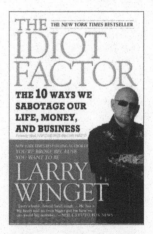

The dumb things people do to sabotage their success, and sound, simple solutions

GOTHAM
BOOKS